Aleta's superpower is supreme listening and the extraordinary ability to show you the path in a way that makes you feel like you found it yourself. But trust me, you didn't. *Women Who Spark* holds the golden ticket to spark your new life journey. Grab it!

~ Katrina Cravy, Speaker and Communications Advisor

This moment is about *you*. Not the roles you fulfill for others, your daily responsibilities, or your busy to-do list. This moment, right now, you are taking the first step to make *you* your priority. As you sit down in a comfortable chair and open Aleta Norris's *Women Who Spark*, you are beginning a sacred journey within. Aleta has provided you with everything you need to discover what makes you spark, set your soul aflame, and light up your life with a new sense of passion, purpose, confidence, and self-care. *Women Who Spark* is a critical guide for every woman who feels burnt out, stuck, and ready for more than the same-old, same-old. Aleta provides you with thought-provoking self-assessments that help you rediscover who you are and what you want, exercises that foster compassion for yourself and others, and words of wisdom and affirmation that enable you to take positive action toward your goals and dreams. Aleta writes with authenticity and vulnerability, sharing her own struggles along her path to finding and owning her spark. *Women Who Spark* will inspire and motivate you and fill you with a renewed optimism and zest for your life!

~ Dr. Colleen Georges, Coach, Speaker,
& Author of the best-selling RESCRIPT the
Story You're Telling Yourself

Aleta operates from the source of love. She is patient and kind, yet thorough. I was a mess. My life was a mess, but I am a better person today because of Aleta. My life, career, and goals are clearly mapped out for me based on my desires, and Aleta is the reason for that. *Women Who Spark* is your self-guided journey.

~ Aziza Letherwood, Talent Manager

If you are struggling to remember who you are, how to be happy, what your purpose is, or how to shine your light on others, *Women Who Spark* is a must read for you. Author Aleta Norris gently, yet firmly, will guide you from confused and complacent to a place of understanding. You will come to embrace your identity, recognize your strengths, and use them to bless the world. I loved this book and was able to read it all in one afternoon. It is easily digestible, empowering, and helps you know that you are not alone. No matter what state or situation you are currently living in, the 12 practical steps in Aleta's book will help you change your life for the better. I highly recommend this book to anyone wanting to get out of their rut and make an impact in the world.

~ Nichole Clark, Founder of More Than Moms &
Author of *The 10-Minute Refresh for Moms*

Women Who Spark is a blueprint for living a positive life. Aleta has a positive outlook on the things in life that get you stuck. Her own life experiences give her an edge. She is committed to helping you find inner peace and happiness, coping amidst the chaos that life throws at you.

~ Leslie Meganck, Retired Nurse

If you want to be inspired, *Women Who Spark* will "spark you" regardless where you are on your journey. Through the words of her book, Aleta will support you, love you and push you to be your absolute best. And if you have the chance, work with her. You can always count on Aleta telling the truth. When it's hard, when it's easy, when it's uncomfortable. She will never take the simple route; she will never be dishonest with you or disregard. I am blessed to have worked with Aleta and personally have shared our journey together for over sixteen years. Words could never describe all the ways in which she has helped me both in my career and in raising my girls as an only parent.

~ Kathleen O'Leary, CEO, Wisconsin State Fair

Aleta is a woman of so many talents and strengths. Her ability to welcome others and make them feel special is a beautiful thing. Aleta's passion for encouraging and supporting women brings joy and fulfillment to everyone who crosses her path. *Women Who Spark* captures the essence of these things.

I have known Aleta for over twenty-five years. She is a dear and trusted friend, business partner and very special confidante. Aleta's warmth and care for others and non-judgmental support is amazing. I love and adore and also respect Aleta to the ends of the earth! I trust her with my life, the life of my family and the care of all things at all times for us all.

~ Nancy Lewis, friend and business partner
at Living As A Leader

Aleta Norris helps shatter the power and weight of the lies that hold many women hostage, the ones that keep them from finding their true happiness. In her book, *Women Who Spark,* she equips you with a set of tools to help you work through life's letdowns and obstacles. Aleta wraps her arms around you and takes you on this journey with her. Through the storytelling of her own life's highs and lows, along with many years of the hands-on and practical coaching she's provided to hundreds of clients, Aleta tells you what you need to hear, motivates you to take the steps necessary, challenges you along the way, walks the journey with you and meets you at the finish line of true happiness and fulfillment in your life. I encourage every woman to read this book. If that were to happen, we'd have a world full of confident, content and calm women.

~ Theresa Custer, friend and associate
at Living As A Leader

Women have a way of competing with one another, comparing different lifestyles and judging those who don't share their same choices. We tear one another down and break into camps of stay-at-home vs. working mom, entrepreneur vs. corporate leader, wife and mother versus single career woman. Aleta unifies all women through her words and processes and empowers each by giving exercises for every woman to find a spark in her own life. She's a leader—wholly gifted at pointing others to their purposes. Aleta has provided a roadmap to identify, focus on, and strengthen things that bring joy to each individual, no matter their backgrounds, lifestyles, or philosophies. She encourages with a combination of hard truths and soft hearts. You'll be proud to know her, and—more importantly, through her book—you'll learn to SPARK:

~ Reji Laberje, Owner of Bucket List to Bookshelf
10-Time #1 International Bestselling Author

What does her own family have to say?

Driven. Strong. Genuine. Hard working. Caring. Understanding. Patient. Mom. Friend. If she's not working behind her laptop, she's cooking in the kitchen, planting flowers in the garden, tidying up the house, walking the dog, or making sure whoever is around the house has what they need.

As someone who owns a successful business and is on her way to running another (*Women Who Spark!*), she still has a way of making her family a priority. If I need someone to talk to or have a glass of wine with, she is there. If I make a mistake, she remains supportive and never judges. If I'm in a tough spot, she's there to talk through it and provide guidance. I'm lucky to call her my mom and, even more than that, my friend.

~ Jaimie Kotlarek, Aleta's Daughter

If you're looking for a guide to a happier life, you've found it here in *Women Who Spark*. Though my mom made sure to keep the hard times to herself during our childhood—to make sure we were taken care of—she navigated the ups and downs without skipping a beat. Today, it's safe to say, she is flourishing in her own life while making the lives better of everyone lucky enough to know her, including me.

~ Steph Kotlarek, Aleta's Daughter

Always the first to rise, Aleta will make you a gourmet espresso before you've managed to wipe the sleep from your eyes. And she will do it with warmth, grace, and generosity.

~ Haley Palec, Aleta's Stepdaughter

I know that I can always count on Aleta to be genuine, with an empathetic voice of reason in any situation. Aleta is a great inspiration as a dedicated career woman, and her strong work ethic never ceases to amaze me! In *Women Who Spark,* she equips all women with the inspiration to work hard and remain calm…a great combination.

~ Kelsey Kotlarek, Aleta's Daughter-in-law

My mom is a *Woman Who Sparks.* One thing that sticks out to me as I look back on our childhood, following my parents' divorce: I cannot remember one time where my mom and dad had a negative exchange—not one. I never saw them have an argument, and my mom has never had a bad thing to say about my dad. I cannot tell you how much I appreciate that as an adult.

~ Ben Kotlarek, Aleta's Son

I struggle to put 50 years of knowing Aleta, my sister, into a few sentences! What I can attest to is that she **is** everything she teaches in this book. She is kind, selfless, genuinely caring, and immensely passionate about helping you become the best person that you can be. From a very young age, and all through her life, life's adversities have only made her a much stronger, wiser person and someone who can relate to the difficulty life can throw at any of us. Love you sis!

~ Sherri Block, Aleta's Sister

WOMEN WHO
SPARK

12 Steps to Catapult Happiness, Cultivate Confidence, and Discover the Purpose of Your Life

ALETA NORRIS

Printed in the United States of America

Published by Author Academy Elite
P.O. Box 43, Powell, OH 43035
AuthorAcademyElite.com

Visit the author's website at www.aletanorris.com

For quantity orders, please contact me directly at

aleta@aletanorris.com

Paperback ISBN-13:978-1-64085-551-9
Hardcover ISBN-13:978-1-64085-552-6
Library of Congress Control Number: 2019930311

Editing by: Teri Capshaw

DEDICATION

To my grandparents, Loren and Bertha Mae, for teaching me kindness and service to others. I treasure my many years with you, especially as a little girl, and I miss you immeasurably.

To my husband, Steve, for being my best guy ever. Thank you for letting me completely be me . . . and for letting it be okay that I don't return that favor to you.

To my "original" three children, Jaimie, Ben, and Steph, for the absolute joy of raising you into adulthood. I am beyond grateful to be your mom.

To Joe and Haley, for rounding out my family to be the large family I dreamed of having. You have added to my joy.

To my dad, for being my first example of a kind, gracious, courageous single parent.

"It all starts with a SPARK!"
~ Aleta Norris

TABLE OF CONTENTS

PART I: YOUR FOUNDATION

PART II: FIND YOUR SPARKS

PART III: MAKE EVERYTHING BRIGHTER

PART IV: DISCOVER YOUR BIGGER PURPOSE

FOREWORD

I first met Aleta in 2006 when she came to California to spend two full days with me doing her LifePlan. She had read my book, *Pathway to Purpose for Women: Connecting Your To-Do List, Your Passions, and God's Purposes for Your Life*, and was in search of the spark she had lost when life circumstances stripped away her dreams. My book had introduced the question, *"What is the connection between my life purposes and the daily existence I am living now?"*—*but* she wanted to meet privately about how to live well in the *ordinary* day-to-day, while also experiencing broader significance. She knew that she needed to put her past behind, pursue peace, find courage, and surrender to God if she wanted to be all he created her to be!

Aleta had so much on her mind when I picked her up for our get-acquainted dinner the evening before our two-day sessions began, but the first thing I noticed was that she was not one to feel sorry for herself. In our time together, she indicated that she was ready to explore all spiritual, personal, and professional growth necessary to accomplish her ultimate goal, which was to showcase God's faithfulness through all her varied trials and bring glory to him while sharing her journey with others.

In 2007, when I launched my inaugural group of Life Purpose Coach® trainees through *Life Purpose Coaching Centers International®*, I was delighted that Aleta joined us for purpose-coaching certification. She showed up with her signature blend of calmness, kindness, and compassion—paired with a pragmatic, no-nonsense approach of steering toward tangible outcomes.

Aleta fully embraced that coaching process and became ready to live out her God-given purpose in life, namely to be an encourager of women, to be one who sparks joy in herself and the lives of others. Is it an accident that, right now, you're reading her book, *Women Who Spark*, or is it more likely that God has created her to bless you?

I love this gal to pieces for, not only rising above her struggles and allowing God to turn her life into something beautiful, but also using her experiences to help others rise above their circumstances. I hope that one day you will have the privilege of calling Aleta "friend," as I do. Connect with her and your life will be changed forever. Tap into the tremendous gifts God has entrusted to Aleta to help you live your best life.

Katie Brazelton, PhD
Author of books on the topic of God's Plan
for our lives, including *Pathway to Purpose*,
Praying for Purpose, *Conversations on Purpose*,
Character Makeover, and Live Big.

INTRODUCTION

As you look around, does it appear that other women's lives are running more smoothly, and perhaps more happily, than yours?

Are you struggling to manage everything happening in your life?

Do you sometimes feel that everyone else's dreams are coming true, exactly the way they've imagined, while yours are not? Their careers are on track, their work is meaningful, their families are happy and healthy, their relationships are solid, and they're fit, energized, and fulfilled in every way?

You are not alone.

Many women I talk to are struggling in one of these ways. And, with so many balls to juggle, it's easy to feel stretched thin. A friend of mine shared recently, "I was

> "The consensus among us: We're underwhelmed by where we are going — and overwhelmed by where we are today."

with a group of girlfriends all weekend and we talked about these exact concerns. The consensus among us: We're underwhelmed by where we are going—and overwhelmed by where we are today."

Do you relate to this struggle?

I want to assure you that what you're feeling is normal, but it doesn't have to be this way.

Like you, I have been on a journey to live a happy, fulfilling life. I have tried to, as effectively as possible, juggle many things and face the unexpected imperfections of life with as much grace as possible.

While I struggled to balance everything, I often looked around and envied the women who had a more put-together life and an easier set of circumstances. The irony was in the number of women who, I came to learn, looked at me as the put-together one.

I wrote this book because I know we are the same, and I want to provide encouragement and camaraderie.

In this book, you will learn how to find greater happiness and confidence while meeting your daily demands—and you'll be challenged to go after *your spark*.

Your *spark*?

You will know if you have it. It's about being *on fire*. When you have a spark, you are confident, happy, and doing things to support your purpose or passion in the world. You're doing things you love and impacting the lives of others. You're excited to wake up and get your day started. You have somewhere to go, things to do, people to affect, dreams to advance . . . and, you need more hours in your day because you don't want to stop.

Are you ready to meet this new version of you—this woman who lights up a room the moment she steps through the door? It's time to get to work.

When you do the work contained in each chapter of this book, you will begin to tame the whirlwind that's tearing through your life. You will develop a plan to change the things you can control—and to *spark anyway* when you can't make a situation better.

When you know who you are and what you're supposed to be doing with your life, you'll also be able to break free from the "comparison game" trap. You know that feeling you get when you're scrolling through your Facebook newsfeed looking at carefully curated "candid" photos of others? It can feel like some people have everything and it comes so easily to them. Do you catch yourself daydreaming?

If only I could be more like them. If only I could be that happy, confident, and sure of myself. What would that be like? Is that even possible?

That's the comparison game trap and your daydream is where you might be wrong. The women you respect and admire (and, perhaps, envy) are likely struggling, too.

This book is for you if:

- You wonder if there is something more to life than what you have going on right now.

- You sense a lack of purpose or direction in your days.

- You reflect on your past with some regret for decisions you've made.

- Your life isn't coming together like you thought it would.

- You're overwhelmed.

- You struggle with self-doubt and insecurity.

- You look around and feel like everyone is happier than you.

- You see other women doing things they love, and you believe you could never have what they have.

If any of these things resonate with you, you are not alone. Public personas very often do not match private battles.

> "Public personas very often do not match private battles."

When you gain the confidence to stop looking around—and start working on you—everything will change. You will no longer feel lonely in a room full of people. You will be able to ask for and accept help without feeling like a failure. You will start doing what's best for you—and everyone around you will benefit as you grow.

PART I

YOUR FOUNDATION

SPARK NOTE!
Ignite On: Knowing Yourself

"When I was a very young girl, my mom always said, 'Liking others has to start with liking yourself. Wow! She was so wise."

~ Nancy Lewis

STEP ONE

GET TO KNOW YOURSELF

In order to go after the life you want to lead, you need to answer this question: Who am I?

It sounds simple, but it's incredibly important. Without a solid sense of self, you may spend your life focusing on what others want from you. You might already be experiencing that self-sacrifice.

Can you relate to any of the statements below?

- I don't even know who I am anymore.
- I've been so busy being what everyone else needs, I've lost my own voice.
- I'm going through the motions.
- Somewhere along the way, I stopped thinking about myself.

- I don't know what I'm supposed to be doing.

- I look in the mirror and I don't see what I want to see.

- I prioritize others, but I don't prioritize myself.

Knowing who you are is essential to leading a happy, confident, purpose-driven life. At the same time, it can feel overwhelming—maybe even intimidating—to dig into deep questions about your identity. But I want to encourage you: you can do this . . . and I can help.

In this chapter, we will take a look at who you are, who you want to be, and how other people see you. Doing the work below is your first step toward becoming a woman who sparks.

Discover Who You Are

How do you show up in the world? In other words, take a moment to focus on the experiences other people have when they are with you. This is a critical focal point, because understanding how you appear to others provides important information about how your actual behavior may differ from your good intentions. Once you know how others perceive you, you'll be able to figure out whether you are being your best true self or you have something to change for that purpose.

You can begin to connect with who you are—and how you appear to the world—in three ways:

1. Be Quiet

When you are in your car, turn off the radio. When you're taking your dog for a walk, leave your earbuds at home. In a noisy world, it's important to find opportunities to be silent, think, and reflect. Replay situations with others in your mind.

What do you notice about yourself? What do others think of you? What do they like? What do they not like?

> "In a noisy world, it's important to find opportunities to be silent, think, and reflect."

As you reflect, think about the women you know who light up a room when they walk through the door. Everyone is happy to see them. They are engaging, encouraging, and interested in others. They have a positive outlook. Are there ways you can be more like those women, while still being true to yourself? You aren't necessarily trying to *act* like them. Instead, think about ways you can use your own personality strengths to make other people around you feel amazing about themselves.

Now think about women who have the opposite effect. Who are those women for you? Are those the women who gossip or talk about others negatively? Is it those who bring an aura of jealousy or criticism? What characteristics do you find to be a negative drain in a room? Perhaps the women who bring these experiences are unhappy themselves and struggling to bring joy to their surroundings. When *they* walk into a room, people find themselves on edge. Do you exhibit some of the character traits that are draining even to yourself? What about when you're feeling stressed out? Are there some things you can do to reduce tension for yourself and others?

2. Ask for Feedback

This is a tough one. If you're in a leadership position, it may feel like asking for feedback is a sign of weakness. However, being willing to be humble and learn more about yourself will help you grow stronger—and inspire confidence in the people you lead and interact with on a daily basis.

Your conversation might sound something like this:

"Katie, could I ask you to share some feedback with me. I'd like to get your opinion about a couple of things you like or appreciate about me—assuming there are some—and a couple of things I could work on. Would you be willing to share?"

You'll notice a touch of humor and humility go a long way toward making the conversation less tense. It's also important to make sure you don't argue with those you're getting feedback from. If Katie says, "You can tend to be negative when you talk about other people," your initial instinct may be to get defensive, but a healthier response would be, "Could you tell me more about that?" If you can keep her talking longer, you'll learn a lot more. Many times, people struggle to say exactly what they mean when they are surprised by a question. If you can engage in a meaningful conversation, you may discover communication problems and areas where your intentions are misinterpreted by others.

Also remember to go into this conversation expecting to get some negative feedback or suggestions. Welcome them. If Katie tells you that you talk about other people behind their backs, you can say, "Wow, you're right. I need to stop. Do you have suggestions to remind myself when I'm doing that?" Own it and show a willingness to improve.

Finally, remember when you ask others for feedback you need to be ready to take it. Don't allow yourself to develop hard feelings over something someone said. You asked for feedback. And it's okay if the people around you have held negative views of your behavior. You're about to blow them away by growing, changing, and becoming the woman you are meant to be.

3. Invest in Personal and Professional Development

I can't imagine growing as a person without the help of talented authors, speakers, and trainers supporting me in my journey. I learn so much by reading books, attending workshops and conferences, and tuning into YouTube channels and podcasts. There is more to learn about human nature and about the complexities of relationships than we can figure out ourselves. (Be sure to check out AletaNorris.com to connect with me and join a tribe of women committed to personal and professional growth.)

I once had an opportunity to work with twenty-four people from one company who had been in leadership roles for several years without any formal leadership training. In that particular workshop, we talked at length about human nature, thinking of people as people (not as objects), and having regard for individuals. At the end of the workshop, we went around the room to hear each person share something meaningful learned during our time together. One gentleman said, "I am so ashamed of myself for how I have treated people for thirty years. I didn't know any of this. No one ever taught me these things." This was long-overdue development, and it was necessary for growth. I asked him if he would be interested in apologizing to the people he had mistreated over the years. He was so grateful for the idea. Without wasting any time, he embarked on an *apology tour*, surprising many people along the way. The people he talked to were so appreciative of his selfless apology. This experience taught him to be more compassionate with people. He was able to retire a few years later with a clear conscience.

Does that story inspire you? How would being quiet, asking for feedback, and investing in your personal and professional development help you make the world a better place, for both yourself and others?

Where will you begin?

Let's put these three ideas together.

"Tough Love" Turnaround

Years ago, I coached a woman named Elizabeth. People struggled to work with her. You see, Elizabeth was not a nice person—and certainly not a happy one. She felt she knew more than others around her. She was critical, blame oriented, and seldom smiled. A furrowed brow was her style. In most situations, she was unwilling to listen to others' ideas. When things went wrong, she was quick to point her finger at others. It was important to her that others saw her as right.

This may not surprise you, but Elizabeth also had difficult relationships at home. She was often at odds with someone in her family. When we met for her coaching sessions, she used at least a portion of our time to vent and share stories about the injustices that surrounded her.

Because Elizabeth was interested in growing in her career, there were some things she needed to get a handle on. I knew that, but I'm not sure Elizabeth knew that. She needed time to think, get some feedback, and grow as a person.

Unfortunately, Elizabeth was not ready to be quiet and think. She was in a state of denial about herself. She didn't see what others saw. In this case, I decided to start with feedback. With her reluctant permission, we started gathering feedback using an anonymous process.

Elizabeth would have a lot of thinking to do. And her personal development would be more effective if it were launched with an awareness of who she was to others—she needed to have a clear understanding of her starting point.

Going into the process, she said to me, "I know people have a perception I'm difficult to work with." I had known Elizabeth for some time by then and we had a comfortable, honest, and trusting relationship. I said, "I am going to challenge your thinking. Perhaps it's not their perception; perhaps it's their experiences with you." She wasn't thrilled.

Are you familiar with the concept of "360-degree feedback?" This is a process in which a person like Elizabeth receives feedback from others around them. In a work situation, this could be their boss (above), their peer group (equal), and their direct reports (below).

The tricky thing about 360-degree feedback assessments is that people have often been seeing themselves differently than others see them. The reason for this? Most of us view ourselves based upon the *intentions* we have. For example, imagine you wake up every day and intend to be a good person, friendly to others, not wanting to hurt people, wanting to be understood by people, and wanting

> "Most of us view ourselves based upon the *intentions* we have."

to be helpful. Since your intentions are good, it is likely you will think, *I am a good person."*

Research, combined with experience, tells us a different story. Let's test this on you. Think about someone you struggle with. Would it be fair to say your perception of this person is based upon a recent, not-so-great experience? Or maybe it's a pattern or accumulation of behavior over time. If someone loses his or her temper with you, your perception will likely be that this person is not nice. If people don't come through for you at times when you really need them, it's likely you perceive that they can't be counted on. Within their own minds, however, these may simply be "one of those things," and certainly not a reflection of who they really are.

We administered the 360-degree feedback process for Elizabeth. We gathered feedback from about twenty people. The results were devastating. She was not prepared for the negative perspectives and experiences people shared about their relationships with her. They viewed her as unfriendly, unhelpful, arrogant, self-centered, blame-oriented, insensitive, and aloof. As difficult as this feedback was for Elizabeth to receive, it served as a wake-up call.

She was ready to be quiet and reflect. To rephrase that, I asked her to be quiet and reflect. She was extremely uncomfortable for several days. She eventually became ready to do the hard work to grow as a person. She also became more concerned about how she was affecting others, rather than focusing on protecting herself. Once she embraced personal development, she began to make noticeable progress.

You may have a more positive outlook on life than Elizabeth did, but all of us have areas where we can improve. In almost every 360 I've done for women over the years, there is something negative that shows up regularly.

Do you tend to exhibit any of these characteristics?

- You withdraw.

- You become aggressive in your demands.

- You get emotional.

- You are argumentative.

- You hold a grudge.

- You avoid difficult conversations.

- You are impatient.

- You don't hold people accountable.

We all have something we can improve upon. Knowing *where* to improve is key. If you don't know what your shortcomings are, you have a blind spot. Your blind spots may be the things between your current reality and getting to a place where you can be a woman who sparks.

Dig Deeper

Use the exercise on the following pages to compare your self-perceptions (the way you see yourself) with the perceptions you believe others have of you.

As you consider your own self-perception, think about your behaviors when things are going well and how you perform on an average day. Then compare that to situations when you are under stress or when things are not going your way. Maybe a co-worker missed a deadline, your kids are not getting out of bed to get ready for school, your spouse is more interested in the football game than listening to you, your server forgot to bring you the water you asked for, or a friend let you down when you needed her. Do you find yourself reacting negatively in any of these situations? Do you judge your co-worker harshly? Do you yell at the kids? Do you go on a tirade with your husband? Do you flag the server down with intolerance? Do you show your frustration with the employee at work?

Human nature is such that your perception of yourself will be most closely related to your intentions and to the positive behaviors you see within yourself. The perceptions others have of you will be most closely related to their experiences with your negative behavior.

As you make your way to a life that sparks in this book, there will be exercises, journaling opportunities, reflective questions, checklists, and other chances to interact and grow through the steps.

This first exercise will give you an opportunity to find your starting point, so you can grow as you work through the rest of this book.

For printable, full-page renderings of these offerings, you can download the free PDF "Women Who Spark Resources Guide" at the Women Who Spark Books website:

www.womenwhosparkbooks.com.

Reflect

Starting with your own self-perception, name three to five words you would use to describe yourself when things are going well and you are at your best.

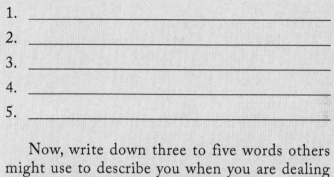

1. _____
2. _____
3. _____
4. _____
5. _____

Now, write down three to five words others might use to describe you when you are dealing with frustrations. It may help if you reflect on some recent frustrating moments with family members, co-workers, or friends.

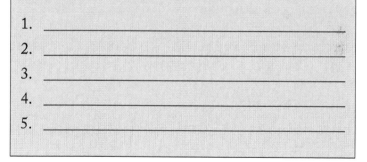

1. _____
2. _____
3. _____
4. _____
5. _____

I know this exercise can be difficult. Many women find it challenging to come up with the right words. You might be thinking, *'I don't know. You'll have to ask other people.'* You can certainly do that. I encourage you, however, to find that quiet time to reflect. Become skilled in knowing who you are.

As I went through this exercise myself, I realized that I see myself as patient, calm, understanding, kind and happy. Others, who endure moments with me when things are not going well, might say I'm intolerant, detached, impatient, cavalier and dismissive. Both sets of words can be true at times. These things are influenced by my internal belief that everything will ultimately be okay, so let's move forward and take the first step.

I've always been an "Ah, just spit on it, rub some dirt on it, and you'll be fine" kind of person. What's important is knowing how your personality might affect others. Since I know that I'm sometimes not good at expressing empathy, I can watch for situations when I may come across the wrong way.

Building upon this idea of self-perception—and to help you in the exercise—let's approach this another way. On the next page is a list of personal qualities and behaviors. For each pair, select the word you believe is the most accurate representation of you, day in and day out. Feel free to skip any along the way if you feel stuck. Sometimes you may think, *'It depends.'* In those cases, choose the word you think others would be most likely to use when describing you. Or select the quality or behavior most likely to show up more than half the time—particularly if you're frustrated.

> "What's important is knowing how your personality might affect others."

Rude	Considerate	Selfish	Thankful	Grumpy	Joyful
Impatient	Patient	Ungrateful	Grateful	Disorganized	Organized
Angry	Pleasant	Blame Oriented	Gracious	Unreliable	Reliable
Interruptive	Good Listener	Unpleasant	Pleasant	Lazy	Hard Working
Emotional	Calm	Critical	Affirming	Immature	Mature
Gossipy	Not Gossipy	Aloof	Welcoming	Unkind	Kind
Judgmental	Non-Judgmental	Defend Your Actions	Own Your Actions	Dishonest	Honest
Loud	Quiet	Discouraging	Motivating	Messy	Neat
Critical	Encouraging	Chaotic	Poised	Sulky	Joyful
Moody	Even Tempered	Apathetic	Caring	Aggressive	Assertive
Sad	Happy	Arrogant	Humble	Unhelpful	Helpful

What do you think of your results? Are you happy with some things, but others make you cringe? If so, you're normal.

As you reflect on the words you circled, think about what they have to say about the impact you have on the world. Your goal needs to be to encourage others and help them experience more joy in life.

Does it sound like I am imposing this on you? I am. You cannot have happiness and confidence if you do not contribute positively to others. If you *do* have happiness and confidence while adversely affecting others, I would argue that your happiness is on the surface ... and your confidence comes with a price. Or it's a façade.

Give Yourself a Break

We've been tackling some tough concepts in this chapter. Now I want you to take a moment to consider some of the reasons you may be struggling in certain areas. Do you tend to lash out at others because you are overwhelmed, stressed out, and frustrated? As we move through this book, I'm going to encourage you to find ways to "tame the whirlwind" in your life. Sometimes that will involve saying "no" to things you should not be taking on. Other times it will mean coming to terms with things you cannot change. In this first step, I want you to start focusing more on how your behavior affects others. I also want you to spend less time worrying about what others think about you. The difference between these two concepts may seem nuanced, but the impact on your life can be significant.

I know far too many women who allow what others *might think* rule their lives. Living with a sense of fear or self-doubt due to a lack of acceptance and affirmation from others will make it difficult for you to be a happy, fulfilled woman who sparks joy in those around her.

Do thoughts like these play repeatedly in your mind?

- But, what will they think?
- I wonder if they'll like me.
- If I do that, people will think I'm crazy.
- I wonder what people will say.

I remember struggling with these kinds of thoughts when I was contemplating my second divorce. At the time, I was lost inside a marriage to a man who struggled with alcoholism and, most importantly, who refused to get help. I was so focused on not triggering his abusive tendencies that I wasn't thinking clearly. I stayed longer than I should have because I was caught up in wondering what others would think.

Have you ever been trapped in a mess in your own life? Have you allowed the fear of what others think to paralyze you when you've needed to take action? When I finally drummed up the courage to get out of my bad situation, I was so surprised. The people I thought would judge me were supportive. Many times, we don't give other people enough credit. (They also have their own situations to worry about.)

I recently came across a stack of cards I received during that difficult season. The support from women around me was heartfelt. They were uplifting and encouraging. And, there were women available to help in any way I needed.

Getting through a difficult situation can also help you begin to see yourself more clearly to decide what kind of impact you want to have on the world.

After that divorce, I started asking myself some serious questions.

WHO AM I?

What is my purpose?

WHAT AM I PASSIONATE ABOUT?

How can I RECAPTURE my joy?

What do I need to do to strengthen my professional success?

What role can friends play in my life?

What are my **INTERESTS**?

HOW DO I IMPACT OTHERS?

What will my LEGACY be?

How can I **STOP** feeling sorry for MYSELF?

How can I shift my focus *away from* loneliness and **FEAR**?

If I could find the answers to these questions, it felt like I could make a bigger difference in the world. I no longer wanted to use my precious energy to merely survive each day. I wanted to use it to thrive. Fifteen years later, I continue to ponder these questions. I never stop asking, thinking, and growing.

Your Day-To-Day Impact on Others

One way we can grow as women is to view our relationships as a series of one-to-one encounters. Each encounter, including the words we speak, will have an impact on our relationship, either positive or negative.

You can use a simple concept I call "above-the-line and below-the-line" to measure the experience others have with you on a daily basis.

Above-the-line interactions add positivity to others' lives and to your relationships with them. Below-the-line interactions add feelings of negativity. Assuming everyone is at a neutral point when they begin an interaction with you, does your interaction add positivity, almost like a deposit, to their lives? Or does it add negativity, like a withdrawal, to their lives? And how about for yourself? Even if no one else is in the room, do you help yourself feel better or worse?

↑↑↑ **ABOVE THE LINE IS LIKE A DEPOSIT** ↑↑↑

↓↓↓ **BELOW THE LINE IS LIKE A WITHDRAWAL** ↓↓↓

Below is a list of common interactions that would tend to add positivity to your life and to the lives of others. These are what I would label as above-the-line interactions. Put a checkmark by the ones that are typical for you:

☐ Say "good morning" with a smile.

☐ Greet people by name.

☐ Even when the checkout person does not greet you with a smile, greet him or her with a smile.

☐ When the server forgets your water, you might say, "Just a friendly reminder to bring me some water when you have a chance."

☐ If someone is frustrated with you because you dropped the ball on something, you can affirm their "rightness" with a comment like, "You are right, and I'm so sorry. Here is what I can do."

☐ If you're not a morning person, you can still say "good morning" to your family or co-workers with a smile.

☐ If someone is angry toward you, you can choose to remain calm.

☐ If someone is not smiling at you, you could ask, "Is everything okay?" Or, you might simply smile at them.

☐ If someone in line behind you has only one item, you let them go ahead of you.

Now let's look at some common interactions that likely add negativity to your life and the lives of others. These are the below-the-line interactions. These things alone may not devastate people, but life can be hard—you don't know what's going on behind the scenes in another person's world.

Put a checkmark by the responses that may be typical for you:

☐ You do not say "good morning" to people.

☐ You do not greet people by name. (This is a missed opportunity to make someone feel valued.)

☐ You may say to a gloomy cashier, "You must be having a bad day." (This one is accompanied by an edge of attitude.)

☐ "Excuse me, my water please?" (Also, with some attitude.)

☐ If someone calls you out, you defend yourself rather than own the problem.

☐ If you're not a morning person, you're grumpy and make it clear to others that you are not a morning person.

☐ If someone is angry toward you, you respond in anger.

☐ If someone is not smiling, you ask, "What's your problem?"

☐ If someone in line behind you has only one item, you pretend like you don't notice.

None of these incidents alone are life altering. They are simple, common, not-a-big-deal moments. However, each negative interaction can feel like a pinch. We all get pinched plenty of times a day. You can choose to light up someone's day instead.

As we move forward, it's important for you to know who you want to be and how you want to impact the world around you. How do you want to affect the lives of people in your life, including people you don't even know? What legacy do you want to leave behind?

Commit to becoming an improved person today by filling in the blank line below:

I am someone who_____.

Spark Note!

Ignite On: The Past's Purpose

"Once in a while, I do think about my own confidence. Really, I think over the years, I have learned through trials, successes, challenges, and failures to become confident."

~ Shay Givans

STEP TWO
LOOK BACK SO YOU CAN MOVE FORWARD

You are not your past.

Well, at least not the not-so-great stuff. You are definitely the good stuff. And as we move forward, do not forget that part of you.

If you are like most women, thinking about some parts of your past is a cringe-inducing experience. But you absolutely need to go there in order to move forward. Processing some of the things you've done—and things that have been done to you—is an essential step in the process of discovering a new, more confident, happier version of yourself. You can do this.

Identify Your Pain Points

☐ Are you paralyzed by past experiences?

☐ Did you struggle as a child to receive approval from at least one parent?

☐ Did you have a sibling who was the favorite?

☐ Have you made decisions that you regret?

☐ Do you sometimes feel hopeless and helpless because you are not where you want to be?

☐ Are you discouraged that you don't make enough money or that you haven't saved enough money?

☐ Are you upset with yourself for getting out of shape?

☐ Is a mean comment from years and years ago still stuck in your brain?

☐ Are you struggling to forgive yourself for something you've done? Or is there something you didn't do?

☐ Are you mad at yourself for choosing a profession you find unfulfilling?

☐ Are you disappointed because your career has been impacted by things outside of your control?

☐ Are you kicking yourself because you spent your money having fun along the way and now have to continue working as some of your friends are moving into retirement?

☐ Have past relationships derailed you?

☐ Do you regret not making amends with a loved one before he or she died?

☐ Do you wish you had finished college?

☐ Are you upset with yourself for wasting away your childhood? Twenties? Thirties? ANY years?"

In *Woulda, Coulda, Shoulda: Overcoming Regrets, Mistakes, and Missed Opportunities,* Authors Dr. Arthur Freeman and Rose Wolf tell us that dwelling on past experiences prevents us from experiencing pleasure in the present. Rather than asking, *"Why?"* we should be asking, *"What next?"* You can't spark if you're stuck in the past. Instead, figure out how you can make the most of what you've learned, look for new opportunities, and find hope in life's possibilities.[1]

Authors Carole Klein and Richard Gotti, PhD also share helpful insights in *Overcoming Regret: Lessons From The Roads Not Taken.* While regret may imply a personal failure, it is a natural and necessary part of life. We all fall short at times. However, if we'll let them, our experiences can fuel future growth. The key is to focus on what comes next rather than dwelling on the past.[2]

After I went through my second divorce, I was in a difficult place. The marriage was a financial disaster. I went to see a financial advisor—and it's almost an understatement to say he reprimanded me. In a raised voice, he said, "You have a fraction of what you should have in investments, you are living a consumption life-style, and you will be in bad shape when you are older if you do not do something." I was so angry with him for what he said, but mostly *how he said it.*

I fumed for a few days and then I jumped into action. I pulled out my journal and documented my current reality. I got on Amazon and ordered a bunch of books about investing. I was filled with regret, fear, and embarrassment—fear most of all. One book gave me the encouragement I needed. In *Start Late, Finish Rich,* author David Bach said:

"Give yourself a break: everyone makes mistakes—smart people learn from them. The fastest way to get rid of regrets is acknowledge them....and burn them up. It's never too late to start."[3]

I needed encouragement and his words helped. I was ready to start clawing my way to a better place.

By the way, I didn't go back to that financial advisor. Even though I needed his message at the time, I didn't have the strength to be demeaned in the process of trying to improve. I vowed I would never use an approach like that in my conversations with another human being. Tough love is good but demeaning and diminishing others for their place in life, not so much.

Almost all women I know have encountered tough circumstances in their pasts. Those difficult times can affect your thinking and fill you with self-doubt, low self-esteem, and self-limiting beliefs.

Do you struggle with any of the thoughts below?

- ☐ I'm not pretty enough.
- ☐ I'm not smart enough.
- ☐ I'm not talented enough.
- ☐ I'm not thin enough.
- ☐ I'll never have a job I love.
- ☐ I don't have any friends.
- ☐ I'm not likable.
- ☐ I'll never amount to anything.

How many of these beliefs are tied to what other people have done or said to you? If you're consumed with memories of things that have been said, it's time to let them go. Don't allow your value as a person to be defined by a conversation from your past. You are now in the business of building a bright future for yourself and improving the experience of everyone who interacts with you. The only thing you need to carry forward from your past is wisdom gleaned from some of your most trying experiences.

Let's pause and take inventory. I want you to do an above-the-line, below-the-line exercise, looking back over your life, decade by decade. The purpose of this activity is to help you see where you've come from so you'll be able to better articulate where you want to go in the future.

I understand if you're not a "do work in a book" kind of woman. Can I push you? You're on a quest to become a *woman who sparks,* and I am confident you will be more successful if you do the work. It may help to find a place where you're comfortable and can focus. Find a pen you love or sharpen a new pencil. Make a hot cup of tea or pour a glass of your favorite wine. Put on some music. In other words, create an environment that will help you enjoy the experience.

Are you with me? Are you ready to reflect? Remember to use top-of-mind thinking. This means that whatever comes to mind first is the thought to jot down quickly. You don't have to dig deep. Your first instinct is likely the accurate one in a self-reflection exercise. You're not in therapy right now. You're in a creative thinking mode. You're simply trying to get a handle on some of the things that have contributed to who you are today—so you can plan for the future.

Okay, let's get started.

Your teenage years:

What good thing(s) happened in your life during this decade?
What do you recall people saying to you that helped fuel your confidence?

↑
_____
↓

What difficult thing(s) happened in your life during this decade?
What do you recall people saying to you that chipped away at your confidence?

Your twenties:

What good thing(s) happened in your life during this decade?
What do you recall people saying to you that helped fuel your confidence?

↑
_____
↓

What difficult thing(s) happened in your life during this decade?
What do you recall people saying to you that chipped away at your confidence?

Your thirties:

What good thing(s) happened in your life during this decade?
What do you recall people saying to you that helped fuel your confidence?

↑

_____

↓

What difficult thing(s) happened in your life during this decade?
What do you recall people saying to you that chipped away at your confidence?

Your forties:

What good thing(s) happened in your life during this decade?
What do you recall people saying to you that helped fuel your confidence?

↑

_____

↓

What difficult thing(s) happened in your life during this decade?
What do you recall people saying to you that chipped away at your confidence?

Your fifties:

What good thing(s) happened in your life during this decade?
What do you recall people saying to you that helped fuel your confidence?

↑
_____
↓

What difficult thing(s) happened in your life during this decade?
What do you recall people saying to you that chipped away at your confidence?

I'll stop here. If you're older than fifty, like me, please continue on another piece of paper or in your journal. If you're younger, you can still do this exercise. You may wish to break the questions down into smaller chunks of time, such as five years or—for the lucky woman who is trying to get a handle on life as early as her twenties, you may wish to look at different life seasons, such as your elementary years, middle school years, high school years, college, and early adulthood. The above-the-line and below-the-line exercise can help you become a woman who sparks regardless of when you are starting.

Let's reflect:

- What did you discover about yourself?
- What have you been reminded of?

- Do you have some validation for why you are primarily a joyful person?

- Or perhaps, do you have some validation for why you are struggling?

- Have you had a mostly good life, or have you had your fair share of challenges?

- Where do you want to go from here?

- What will you let go of?

- What and who do you need to find peace with?

- Who do you need to have a conversation with?

- What wisdom gleaned can you leverage for the future?

The Seven Habits of Highly Effective People, by Stephen Covey, has provided a roadmap for many people's lives. In the first habit, "Be Proactive," Covey tells us the serious problem with reactive language is that it becomes a self-fulfilling prophecy. The more we tell ourselves things like, *"There's nothing I can do"*, *"That's the way I am"*, *"I can't"*, *"I must"*, *and "If only,"* the more we can produce evidence to support those things. Unfortunately, beliefs like that make us feel increasingly victimized. Proactive thinking, on the other hand, will lead us to tell ourselves things like, *"I can"*, *"I will"*, *"I choose to"*, *"I will create"*, *and "I prefer."*[4] Proactive thinking helps us take initiative. Reactive thinking can fuel feelings of pain and prompt us to focus on what might have been instead of what is. Proactive thinking will help propel us into a problem-solving and solution-creating mode.

Where will you take initiative? How will you change your thinking?

I know this can be a tough chapter to tackle. When I think about my childhood, I remember the trauma caused when my mom left our family when I was eight-years old. I realize it affected me in adverse ways: I do not have a relationship with my mom, I will likely never know what it feels like to have a mom to turn to, and there are things I did not have role modeled for me or taught to me in a measured, gradual way. I became overly independent and did not learn to negotiate in my relationships. My kids are also affected by not having an involved grandma.

On the other hand, there are ways that difficult experience may have helped me. When my mom left, I jumped into action. I helped my dad around the house and watched my little sister. That traumatic situation helped me grow into a productive and independent young woman. My friends called me a thirty-year old ten-year old. I learned how to do a lot of things I may not have otherwise figured out. My dad was calm, kind, loving, and encouraging. He told me my whole life that I could do whatever I set my mind to. I'm not sure he would have been able to shine in that way if my mom were there.

I encourage you to pause and reflect on what you're still hanging on to from your past experiences. Are you regretful? Resentful? Keeping score? Refusing to let go? Identify a couple of areas where you can be more proactive.

We are all in control of our patterns of thinking. It may not be easy for you to shift from below-the-line thinking to above-the-line, proactive thinking, but it's worth learning to master your mind so it will serve you better in the future. Making peace with your past will be a big step forward.

STEP THREE
UNDERSTAND YOUR ROLES AND RELATIONSHIPS

When you take time to reflect on how things are going—and what needs to change—you are giving yourself an opportunity to take your life to a whole new level.

Have you ever had a disappointing performance review? Or, to put it another way, have you ever experienced an amazing performance review? If not, that's going to change today. Many performance reviews are executed poorly, but the concept behind this is solid. They offer areas to improve and areas where you are doing well that you can maximize on. When you apply those things toward your next-level life, you'll be more confident and prepared to make the most of each day.

What's Working? And What Needs to Change?

Have things been tough lately? Just okay? Neither good nor bad? Do you wake up each morning excited about the day ahead? Let's consider this chapter a performance review of your life where you can take time to get a handle on the many roles and relationships you're juggling.

This is your life.

It doesn't have to be overwhelming. But if you're going to make it amazing, you will have to put in some serious effort and planning. Your life is a major event and I want you to spend more time and energy planning your life than you've ever spent coordinating any other event. Doesn't your life deserve as much?

When you take your future seriously, you can begin creating the environment you need to spark. Authors Bill Burnett and Dave Evans argue that, by adopting the mindset of a designer, you can discover and build a new life or even several of them. In *Designing Your Life: How to Build A Well-Lived, Joyful Life,* they explain that we put as much emphasis on *problem-finding* as we do in *problem-solving.* Creating your ideal life may be as simple as figuring out what you need to get (add) and what you need to get rid of (subtract).[5]

What do you want to make space for in your life? Is it time for a better job? Do you want to earn more money? Or maybe the most important thing right now is developing a better relationship with your spouse. You might also want to challenge yourself by going after a college degree. Or maybe you want to focus on personal growth by cultivating a more adventurous spirit or a greater ability to laugh. Figure out what's going to make a positive difference in your unique life and work to *add* that.

What you get rid of might have an even bigger impact on your life. It might be a task eating up valuable time in your schedule. Or maybe it's something you've never considered changing. Do you have a dramatic friend who is making both of your lives miserable? Is your job draining the life out of you? Or maybe you have a grumpy disposition you need to ditch or *subtract* from your life?

Perhaps you don't even know the answers to these questions. That's fine for now, but you need to find time to figure them out. Life is short and you need to make sure you're spending your time well by coordinating your biggest event—*your life.*

Before writing this book, I asked several dozen women to complete an exercise similar to the one you're about to tackle. The exercise reviews a year-in-the(your)-life looking at three simple questions across ten significant areas. The positive feedback was overwhelming.

The women not only provided information for my research regarding fulfillment and happiness, but they found the process of answering these basic questions about their lives beneficial.

Here are some of the thoughts they shared:

- *I loved the opportunity to put some thought behind this topic. I know change is powerful and a part of life. I used to resist this, but now I think it is healthy and necessary.*

- *I realize I am just trying to get by. That is not good enough. It is good to think about these ten areas.*

- *I liked thinking about these questions. I am studying authenticity and how best to apply my results daily.*

This teaching is valuable and often lost in how we share of ourselves every day.

- *This tool reinforces to me that I want to do more. I want to give more. I want to be more. I don't know if I will ever live the life I am truly meant to live, but I want to try to get there. I want people to stop hurting each other. We are too cruel a society. I want love. I want joy. I want peace.*

- *I am content with my life so far. But I want to stretch and grow until the very end. I don't want to miss anything life has to teach me, so I have to keep paying attention to these things.*

- *Sometimes it takes things like a survey to stop and think and evaluate things for a minute.*

- *I appear confident, but I always second guess myself. I don't feel good enough at times. This exercise shows me that I have work to do.*

- *Oh my gosh, I'm so excited to be doing this. This work is the meat of the exact conversations I and my friends are starting to have with one another. We feel we're at a kind of crossroads. We'd love to have help with this, and this tool is a great place to start.*

Now I want you to dig deep, review your own life, and discover where you want to go in the future. If you don't have time to complete the entire exercise now, take a moment to put it on your schedule.

You can't afford to miss this opportunity!

Review Your Year

I encourage you to carve out about thirty minutes to complete this section. You are welcome to write in your book or you can note this in a journal. If any of these areas of life that I've selected are not relevant, you can skip them.

This is your opportunity to take a broad look at your life. Identify and celebrate the areas where you're happy, fulfilled, and doing well. Also make sure you find areas where you're struggling and need to take a better approach.

For each of the ten areas, you will answer three questions:

1. What is going well for you in this area of your life?

2. What is not going as well as you would like?

3. On a scale of 1 - 3, what satisfaction score would you give this area of your life?

    a. 3 = I'm very happy with this area of my life

    b. 2 = I'm happy enough

    c. 1 = I'm not very happy about this area of my life

As in the previous exercise, try to not overthink your answers. You can quickly jot down a satisfaction score followed by a few things that easily come to mind.

If you're struggling to complete this exercise, try the following strategies:

- Tackle one section per day until you've gone through all of them.

- Instead of being tied to the pages of this book, treat yourself to a pretty, lovely, inspiring journal. I don't know about you, but I'm inspired when my writing supplies are beautiful.

- Do this work in a different format. Download the Women Who Spark Resources Guide at www.womenwhosparkbooks.com.

YOUR RELATIONSHIP WITH YOUR SPOUSE OR SIGNFICANT OTHER	Satisfaction:
What is going well for you in this area of your life?	
What is not going as well as you would like?	

FAMILY (immediate or extended)	Satisfaction:

What is going well for you in this area of your life?

What is not going as well as you would like?

FRIENDSHIPS	Satisfaction:

What is going well for you in this area of your life?

What is not going as well as you would like?

HEALTH AND FITNESS	Satisfaction:

What is going well for you in this area of your life?

What is not going as well as you would like?

SPIRITUALITY, JOY, PEACE, CONTENTMENT	Satisfaction:
What is going well for you in this area of your life?	
What is not going as well as you would like?	

HOME AND SPACE	Satisfaction:
What is going well for you in this area of your life?	
What is not going as well as you would like?	

HOBBIES AND INTERESTS	Satisfaction:
What is going well for you in this area of your life?	
What is not going as well as you would like?	

FINANCES	Satisfaction:
What is going well for you in this area of your life?	
What is not going as well as you would like?	

WORK AND PROFESSIONAL LIFE	Satisfaction:
What is going well for you in this area of your life?	
What is not going as well as you would like?	

MOM ROLE	Satisfaction:
What is going well for you in this area of your life?	
What is not going as well as you would like?	

I know this analysis is hard work, but you and your spark are so worth the effort.

Now that you've considered how things are going in several life categories above, it's time to summarize what you've learned.

Summary of the year:

What are the three areas that are going the best for you?

1.

2.

3.

What are the three areas that are most disappointing for you?

1.

2.

3.

What are three areas you feel most committed to focusing on in the coming year?

1.

2.

3.

Great work. You are on track to discover how to become a happy, confident woman. Now, let's move onto the fun stuff. The next three steps are designed to help you find your sparks.

Spark **Note!**

Ignite On: Passion

"My passion is helping people feel good. I love creating special moments, making people laugh, helping them reconnect and remember that they're beautiful and loved."

~ Tiffany Kells

PART II
FIND YOUR SPARKS

Spark **Note!**

Ignite On: Everyday Joys

"As a woman, I have so much gratitude. I chose to pursue an advanced
education where others cannot. I can
work and worship as I choose. My
body is mine and I may speak my
thoughts. I am so fortunate to be able
to choose my work, my marriage, my
friends."

~ Mary Thomae

STEP FOUR
Find Happiness in Your Ordinary Day

There is no better time to be happy than right now.

Even so, happiness can seem elusive. If you are like 33% of women, you're probably struggling in this area. *Women Who Spark* decide what they will do to create their happiness.

In this chapter we're going to look at ways you can choose to experience more happiness every day.

The Science of Happiness

Amit Sood, M.D., is the author of the Mayo Clinic Handbook for Happiness. In an article about his handbook he wrote, "Half of your happiness depends on conscious choices you make every day — choices that, with time, become habits."[6]

You have an opportunity to change your entire outlook on life. According to Snood, the three most important things you can do include: eating a healthy diet, getting exercise you enjoy, and getting plenty of sleep. In other words, the things you already know you need to prioritize for your health can also help make you happy.

Many times, happiness is a byproduct of something else. Look for opportunities to act in ways that will boost your enjoyment of life. Choose to take an enjoyable walk knowing that the time you spend doing something good for yourself will boost your mood—and affect everyone who interacts with you. Or, if you're feeling a bit "blah," let some friends talk you into a joining them for a fun night out. Spending time doing things with people you enjoy being around will trigger chemicals that help you experience feelings of happiness while making memories.

Develop a Happy Mindset

As a young married woman in my twenties. I put a lot of pressure on my husband to nurture my happiness. I remember being sad and disappointed a lot. It didn't take much to set me off. It could be something as simple as a passing comment, an omission of attention, or an absence of friendliness. I remember withdrawing during those times.

By the time I was in my early thirties, I had three kids, a fun career, and I was busy in graduate school. I also had my health and lots of friends, yet I continued to struggle with happiness.

I met with a therapist who wanted to go back to the beginning and chat about childhood experiences.

I started by saying, "I had a happy childhood." Then, I shared some specifics.

The therapist said, "You did not have a happy childhood." Seriously, that was the first thing out of his mouth. I remember thinking, '*Who are you to tell me I wasn't happy as a kid? It's a mindset.*' I never returned to that therapist's office.

While I maintained a positive outlook on my childhood, sometimes I wonder what might have been different if I had addressed things openly as a young adult.

Happiness is a personal thing. You *have* to know what makes you feel happy. For me, to be content is to be happy. I have a quiet nature and I am usually happy to be by myself. However, it's important for me to have companionship in my life at the same time. For many years following my divorces (yep, both of them), I was intentional about trying to meet my person, my life companion. While some women are happy to be alone, to fly solo in life, I am wired to be half of a couple. I know that is part of my personal formula for happiness.

During those times I sought greater happiness, I wanted my person. When I found him (and it took me years), I discovered I could then be content when I was alone.

For you, happiness may require something different. Maybe you require adventure, a steady dose of people, laughter, challenging work, excitement, or new experiences. Here's the key: you have to know what will create happiness in your life. And it should be something attainable. Maybe you can have a set of short-term goals you can control to experience happiness on a daily basis while you wait for some bigger things you cannot control to work out in your life.

It is easy to get caught up in the game of *I'll be happy* **when**....

- *I'll be happy* **when** *I meet my special person.*
- *I'll be happy* **when** *I get married.*
- *I'll be happy* **when** *we buy a house.*
- *I'll be happy* **when** *I have a baby.*
- *I'll be happy* **when** *we buy a bigger house.*
- *I'll be happy* **when** *I get a job I like.*
- *I'll be happy* **when** *the kids are in school.*
- *I'll be happy* **when** *the kids are grown up.*
- *I'll be happy* **when** *I can buy the car of my dreams.*
- *I'll be happy* **when** *I retire.*
- *I'll be happy* **when**....

Are you an "I'll be happy when" woman? Are you missing the present as you focus on what could be better in the future?

Stop right now.

Think.

What is one thing you can be happy about in this precise moment? There has to be *one* thing, at least, that you can be happy about. For me it can be as simple as a hot cup of tea, a good book, and a cozy spot on the couch.

Deliberately Happy

One of the books that recently captured my attention is *The Happiness Project,* by Gretchen Rubin. Her "project" is a great example of the ways in which we can own our own happiness. We can choose to be intentional about it. Gretchen sets the stage for her project by saying "this project is an approach to changing your life." Over the course of twelve months, she set out to identify concrete resolutions for boosting her own happiness.[7] Along the way, by focusing on these simple strategies that she could control, she developed a deeper sense of happiness.

Are you intrigued by this idea? Maybe it's time to experiment with how you can make yourself happier. If you wake up every day with a hollowness or emptiness inside of you, I encourage you to take small steps by doing those things that you can control.

Women who spark are women who *choose* happiness. They create sparks around them, both for themselves and for others. Do you have friends who spark? We might call them sparkly. They bring joy with them everywhere they go.

Let's be honest for a moment about your days. In what ways are you sabotaging yourself? Where are you robbing yourself of your own happiness? When are you grumpy? When are you unfriendly toward other people? How many times a day do you break your promises to yourself? When you're in a funk, do you stay home with your head under the covers?

Lots of things in your environment can contribute to your happiness. Identify what they are and take steps to make sure they're in your life on a regular basis.

Check the things below that could contribute to your happiness, especially if you give them the credit they deserve. Then add your own!

- ☐ Dancing
- ☐ Friends
- ☐ Flowers
- ☐ A hug
- ☐ Volunteering
- ☐ Being kind
- ☐ Success at Work
- ☐ The smell of fresh-cut grass
- ☐ Dinner with friends
- ☐ Laughing
- ☐ Playing music
- ☐ Chocolate
- ☐ Listening to music
- ☐ A morning cup of coffee
- ☐ A great cup of chai tea
- ☐ Time with your pet
- ☐ Watching sports
- ☐ Participating in sports
- ☐ Watching your kids play sports
- ☐ Eating your favorite ice cream

- ☐ Cuddling up with a good book
- ☐ Sleeping in on a Saturday morning
- ☐ Sitting in front of a fire
- ☐ Going to bed with the sound of rain on the roof
- ☐ Walking in a snowstorm
- ☐ Laying in the sun
- ☐ Enjoying a nice glass of wine
- ☐ Binge watching a really great TV series
- ☐ Going to see a movie
- ☐ Putting on your comfy clothes
- ☐ Taking a tropical vacation in February
- ☐ _____
- ☐ _____
- ☐ _____
- ☐ _____

Bright Spots on Bleak Days

Obviously, you're still going to deal with sadness at times. I remember dealing with so many emotions following my second divorce. I was dealing with the effects of two divorces, financial challenges, and trying to get my professional life back onto a strong footing.

During that bleak time, lots of things made me feel happy, including time spent with my kids (which was fortunately a lot), a house full of lit vanilla spice candles, raking leaves in the fall, a fire in the fireplace, a glass of wine with a friend, a good book, and traveling to see my sister. It doesn't matter what it is that makes you happy—what's important is knowing that you *can* still find happiness in the midst of difficulties.

You may also discover that the small things add up to be some of the biggest things over time.

*Happ*iness is a positive emotional reaction to something *happ*ening in our lives. We cannot be happy all of the time. We can, however, experience happiness more often. Remember, you can only live the sparked life if you choose to do so.

Do you choose to take responsibility for your happiness?

SPARK NOTE!

Ignite On: Confidence

"I love myself. That's where my confidence comes from. Self-care is necessary and truly priceless!"

~ Mary Cleveland

STEP FIVE

CULTIVATE CONFIDENCE

We can't talk about happiness without talking about confidence.

Deep, real, authentic happiness requires confidence. Without it, happiness rests on the surface. It is fleeting and fragile. If you lack confidence, your happiness may feel forced and fake—the kind of "happiness" when you put your best foot forward and you smile . . . because you *should*.

> "Deep, real, authentic happiness requires confidence."

When you choose to become *authentically* confident, everyone around you benefits. People miss the real you if you are not able to shine and to be on fire about your purpose in the world. Your confidence and happiness are gifts to everyone around you.

If you struggle in this area, you are not alone. Many women lack confidence—and it can make them feel like they're failing no matter how much they've accomplished in life.

Here are a few examples:

- Recently I had coffee with a woman I've known for years. She is a successful business woman, well known in the community, highly talented, and a strong contributor. She confided in me. "I feel like one day I will be discovered. People will realize I don't know what I'm doing." I've learned enough about women's journeys over the years to not be surprised. I felt sad for her, however, because she is *amazing*. She is an executive and that *is* because she knows what she's doing. And yet, she does not see it.

- A few months ago, another woman whose confidence I have always admired asked for my advice on how to provide feedback to one of her clients. After I shared some ideas, she said, "I don't think I can do that." I never would have imagined.

- Another time, I talked to a senior level executive who struggled with confidence her entire life because of something her father said to her when she was a little girl. I won't repeat the comment, because it is feels inappropriate to share. The essence of the comment, however, was "You are worthless." Sixty years later, she was still paralyzed by those words.

You cannot be happy if you are not confident.

You can smile. You can put on a good front. You can hang in there with the best of them. But you can't have pure, deep, joyful happiness.

Confidence is your belief in yourself. It is your belief that you can figure things out, that you can overcome the things that are put in your path, and that you are as capable and deserving as the person next to you.

You are in charge of your own confidence. You, and you alone, get to decide how you will see yourself. Those words sound so simple and yet we all know it's not easy. In this chapter, your mission is to discover how to be confident, consistently, over time, and in any circumstances.

We'll get started by looking at what gets in the way of our self-worth.

Nix the Six! Eliminate These Common Confidence Busters from Your Life

1. **You are overwhelmed.** It's easy to take too much on. In our society there is a tendency to measure a woman's value by her productivity, as well as the productivity of her children and family as a whole. We get drawn into robust calendars and lots of activity. Unfortunately, that often leads to feeling overwhelmed. When that happens, everything feels like a mess. When things feel like a mess, it is easy to feel incapable—and that leads to a loss of confidence.

2. **You are grappling with guilt or shame.** Is there something from your past you've been holding onto? Do your mistakes continue to haunt you? Are you being too hard on yourself? Guilt related to the actions and decisions of your younger self can get in the way of your confidence today. If you are

struggling to forgive yourself, you may carry this weight around with you for a long time.

3. **You have given others permission to hurt you.** Others' words may also have had a negative impact on your confidence. Words and actions hurt women, and the effects can last a long time. Who has led you to feel shame, a feeling that you are not worthy? Who are you allowing to have power over you?

4. **You compare yourself to others.** A significant portion of your low confidence is probably rooted in comparison. The women around you are smiling, their families are laughing and having fun, their houses are bigger, their jobs are more fulfilling, and they have busy social calendars. Or so it all seems. It is easy to feel like your life is less impressive than someone else's. If you struggle with this, you are not alone. In a world where social media posts and magazine covers stare at us every day, it is no wonder we get lost in our heads wondering how these other women have figured out how to be (or at least appear to be) so confident and happy.

5. **You are stuck in a whirlwind of disappointment.** Disappointment paralyzes many women. We find ourselves obsessing over all of the things that have not gone the way we envisioned. It might be our careers, marriages, or relationships with our kids. It might also be the absence of children, or a lack of friendship or romance. It could be weight, energy, or purpose. The negative effect of disappointment is compounded when we're also caught in the habit of comparison. These two confidence busters work to amplify one another. When you allow this type of thinking (comparison and disappointment) to creep

into your mind, you risk talking yourself into a false belief that your life is a disaster while everyone else has it all figured out. Disappointment is a real and necessary part of life. It in no way indicates failure. It is predictable. Life is too complicated to go well all the time. Obsessing over your disappointments will get you in trouble.

6. **You feel like you're not good enough.** This confidence buster is actually the culmination of the first five things on this list. You are overwhelmed, grappling with guilt and shame, stuck with the verbal abuse of others, comparing yourself to others, and ruminating on disappointments. Of course, you feel like you're not good enough! That is predictable.

There is a reality of course to the fact that some of our confidence is couched in who we are innately. About 50% of women have a genetic disposition toward a stronger sense of self. These are the women who comfortably rely on intuition, they make quicker decisions than others, and they're comfortable taking risks. It is part of their constitution. They have a "natural air" of confidence. To that air, though, these women work to "nix the six" confidence busters. The other half of women were born with a more tentative nature. As such, these women will have a greater reliance on certainty, proof, affirmation, and comfort that they are okay. If you fall into this second group, in addition to working to eliminate confidence *busters*, there are some specific steps you can take to develop life-changing confidence *builders*.

Ten Ways to Cultivate Confidence

1. **View confidence as a journey.** Rather than focusing on your lack of confidence now, focus on what you can do to grow in confidence. With every step you take to master almost anything, your confidence will become stronger. Think about something you do routinely. Now, think back to the first time you did it. You might have been nervous because you didn't know what to expect. The second time was better, and the third time was almost easy. It's common to feel overwhelmed and incapable when you take on a new role. I often tell people, "Just wait. One year from now, you will feel so different about this."

2. **Post affirmations.** Affirmations help you manage your thought patterns. It's easy to get caught up in your head with phrases related to not being good enough, not being able to do what the person next to you is doing, and not being smart enough. You can replace those thoughts with affirming phrases. Look at some options below for ideas—and come up with some of your own. Write a few of your favorites on notecards or sticky notes. Post them where you can see them to remind yourself.

   - I am smart.
   - I am worthy.
   - I am successful.
   - I am likable.
   - I am unique and equally valuable.
   - I deserve to be happy.
   - I can achieve my dreams.
   - I can do this.

3. **Take small steps.** Completing big projects, chasing dreams, and cultivating new talents can feel overwhelming. It is easy to fall into a trap of thinking, "I could never do that." Instead of letting yourself be intimidated by the big picture, find one small step you can take today. For example, if you dream of leaving your job and starting a business, the first step could be to buy a journal to use while you brainstorm your potential business ideas and document what you're learning along the way. The second step could be to create a list of all of the business ideas you have. The third step could be researching information on the internet about how to start a business. Progress cultivates confidence.

4. **Keep your social media feeds in perspective.** One of our biggest comparison traps is social media. Please keep in mind that real life is what happens when the photos are *not* being taken. I have seen many struggling women stop and smile for a photo. As soon as the photo is taken, the smile fades. Not everyone is as happy and put together as their photos suggest. And, regardless of how happy, beautiful, and exciting all of the photos look, almost every woman I have ever met has something that is a struggle.

   Remember, it's likely those women in your social media circles have also been hit with broken dreams and the unforeseen twists and turns of life.

   Instead of allowing yourself to be consumed by a competitive spirit, ask yourself, "I wonder what her struggle is? I wonder what I can't see?" Be realistic and compassionate to her and yourself.

5. **Manage your self-talk.** This is a big one. Imagine you walk into an event attended by people you don't

know. You notice that almost everyone is deep in conversation. No one notices you or welcomes you.

Your self-talk may kick in:

- *'I shouldn't be here.'*
- *'I don't belong.'*
- *'Everyone else here knows someone.'*
- *'The sooner I get out of here the better.'*
- *'What was I thinking?'*

I promise you none of these things are true. Try a little trick: If you are alone, get a beverage, then stand at a high-top table or an off-to-the-side spot in the room. Look around and calmly observe the room. Within about one minute, someone will come and talk with you. This will be a person who arrived alone, like you did. Or it will be a kind person who notices you are alone. Soon, you will be knee deep in a conversation, intimidating the next solo person who arrives. We all want the comfort of being in a conversation. Often, self-talk is based on mistaken beliefs.

When I initially started attending business networking events, my self-talk sounded like this, "Oh boy, what am I doing here? This is really uncomfortable. I think I'll talk to one person, then I'll leave." That was my ticket out the door. The next time I did the same thing. The third time I attended an event, I realized that I knew a small group of people and I challenged myself to meet one more person before I could leave. All of these years later, I know numerous people almost everywhere I go in my business community. My confidence has grown.

Your self-talk will find plenty of opportunities to take you into a rabbit hole of insecurity. Replace it with a strategy.

6. **Focus on others.** This may feel counterintuitive. After all, I've already pointed out that comparison is not a good thing. This is different from comparison. This is about getting outside of your own head and, instead, looking at the positive attributes, activities, and accomplishments of the women around you. Who inspires you? Who do you want to compliment? Who do you want to emulate? What do you want to replicate?

   Focusing on others also includes asking, "What can I do for her?"

   Consider the networking example I shared. Rather than focus on your insecurity, look around the room for another person who is alone. Find ways to put her at ease by starting a conversation. And when you are in a conversation, watch for others who arrive alone. Help minimize their awkward moments.

   As you begin to think more about others, the less you will be focused on your own insecurities and disappointments.

7. **Accept that some fear, insecurity, and self-doubt are normal.** In the 1980s, a professor by the name of Steven C Hayes, introduced us to the idea that some suffering in our lives is inevitable and an essential part of being human. Rather than try to replace all negative thinking with positive affirmations, he suggested we could connect with our thoughts, remind ourselves they are not true, and move on.[8]

Equipped with this information, perhaps you can find some peace when you're tempted to become overwhelmed by fear. One strategy to deal with your inevitable insecurities in a healthy way is to pull out your journal and jot down some of your thoughts. If you can get them out of your head and onto a piece of paper, perhaps you can look at them objectively and move on to something else.

8. **Keep in mind that everyone is afraid.** Most of us are afraid we are not good enough, beautiful enough, successful enough, or capable enough. At times we are all afraid we can't achieve our dreams or do what someone else is doing. Even wildly successful people are afraid.

   The next time you are at an event—let's say a theater or stadium of some kind—look to your right, then look to your left. These people on either side of you may not look afraid, but they are afraid of something. Of what, you ask? The list of possible reasons is endless. They might be afraid of getting old, not having enough money for retirement, not being likable, being lonely when their kids leave home, being unable to pay the rent, not being able to ever have a child, not being able to find a job they will actually love, giving a speech at their daughter's wedding, or that life will never be better than it is right now. Everyone is afraid at times, but you can learn to manage your fears, put them in perspective, and become more confident.

9. **Do something to get yourself unstuck.** If you're stuck dwelling on your fears and your long list of disappointments, *do something*. Don't try to tackle everything all at once. **Do.One.Thing.** Whatever

is swirling in your head, move it from thoughts to paper. Then pick the one thing from that paper that you'll use as a starting point for action. From thoughts, to words, to action. After that action step is accomplished, choose one more thing. Then one more. Each step will move you closer to realizing your dreams. Or choose one disappointment to tackle. Figure your way out of it. Fix it. Make it better. Change your life one step at a time.

- If you're afraid you're not likable, call one friend you feel comfortable with and invite her to have a cup of coffee or a glass of wine with you.
- If you're disappointed your job is not more fulfilling, jump on a job site and see what is out there.
- If you're disappointed your son doesn't call you more often, pick up the phone and call him.
- Do something. Own what you want and go after it.

10. **Create your own definition of who you are and what your life is.** It's easy to get distracted by what everyone else is doing. Instead, design your life. You need to get excited about who you are and what you want your life to be.

> "It's easy to get distracted by what everyone else is doing. Instead, design your life. You need to get excited about who you are and what you want your life to be."

Dedicate this to writing. Who are you? What will you not compromise? What do you feel sure of? What habits and rituals should be a part of your day? What are your dreams? What do you want to accomplish today, this week, this month, this quarter?

When we get to Step Eleven, "Go Get Your Sparks!", we will go deeper into how to make these things happen. When you make the things that are most important to you a priority, you will discover a whole new level of confidence.

STEP SIX
SPARK ANYWAY

Life has a way of stacking up disappointments.

In this chapter we're focusing on how to develop a healthy perspective when dealing with some of our most difficult life experiences. We will discover how disappointments can co-exist with the happier moments of our lives. No matter what, we can lean toward joy.

Remember earlier in the book when I mentioned my mom leaving our family? You would probably think that would be one of my most devastating life experiences. However, at that time, I was resilient. Even though my mom left, for some reason, I was okay. I didn't cry over that experience. Throughout my childhood, my dad told me I was wonderful, that I could one day do whatever I wanted to do. The passion I still have today for purpose is something I think was born of the independence that I had to build out of necessity when my mom left. The experience strengthened me rather than triggered disappointment in me. Disappointment came later in life in a different way.

Truly, my first brush with that emotion was my first marriage. When I got married and had my daughter, I didn't choose to be a stay-at-home mom. It wasn't who I was. My husband was disappointed in my choice. He wondered what was wrong with me. It was difficult for me, because it was the first time I was told that I wasn't enough just being myself. The resilience I experienced when my mom left, followed by the wavering, unconditional support of my dad, did not prepare me for how to handle this later-in-life disappointment when it happened. I didn't handle it well.

Sometimes the impact of others' expectations collide with reality and your prior life experiences. This collision can take you by surprise—and extinguish your sparks. If you're struggling, it doesn't matter if your pain is in the past or the present. Whatever is holding you back now needs to be dealt with so you can spark anyway.

After my mom left, I grew up quickly. I stepped up to the plate and said, "Dad, I'll help take care of things." I enjoyed contributing. I imagine this is why my dad gave me a lot of freedom to do things I wanted to do. As far as kids go, I was pretty laid back. My childhood was easy going, with support from loving grandparents, along with my favorite aunt and uncle.

As I think back to those years, the simplest of things made me happy: Dreamsicles and fudge bars on a hot day, swinging off a rope into the river, fresh fruit at my grandma's, learning how to sew, having a picnic at the zoo, going to the circus, catching fireflies in our pajamas and putting them in a jar, seeing who could spit watermelon seeds the farthest, running through a sprinkler, eating a big bunch of green grapes, and building forts with blankets. While enjoying these simple experiences of happiness, I did not hear the word "no" very often from the kind, supportive extended family I was surrounded by.

When, as an adult, I started hearing things that felt critical, I didn't know what to do. And when I started feeling disappointed, I was at a loss. My need for affirmation, along with my desire to be "free to be me," were factors that led to my first divorce.

The end of eleven years of marriage set in motion fifteen years of what I like to call "desert crossing." This was a series of things that felt challenging and hard: a chaotic second marriage, financial problems, balancing business ownership with being a single mom of three kids, and keeping a household running. I also struggled with loneliness, fear, and regret. And dating? Ah jeez. That could be a book all in itself . . . a book I will likely *not* write.

But there are also some amazing things that happened during those years. There was laughter and the comfort of everyday life with my three kids. There were business milestones met as my business partner and I made a difference in our clients' lives. And walking through some of the darkest days of my life helped me become a stronger and more confident woman.

The hope I want you to see in this story is that it doesn't matter what life throws your way. What's important is how you learn to handle disappointment. We get ourselves into trouble when we carry around our own disappointments while envying the perfect lives we believe others are leading. Everyone has a difficult season (sometimes

> "Everyone is broken by life, but sometimes people are stronger in the broken places."
> ~ Ernest Hemingway

many). The question we each have to emerge with is, "What can I do with this?"

Ernest Hemingway said, "Everyone is broken by life, but sometimes people are stronger in the broken places." It's true; grit and perseverance are born out of difficulty, hardship, and disappointment.

Influence Your Situation

When I spent two days with my coach, Katie Brazelton, she asked me, "How are you not a bitter woman?" Oh gosh, that never crossed my mind. What good would come from being bitter or angry or resentful? I have a knack for ending difficult relationships with grace, moving on, and wishing everyone well. I mean no harm to anyone. That is in my DNA. For all the things I don't have (like perseverance to hang in there through the good times and bad), I do have that bit of graciousness that helps things end calmly.

During my desert-crossing years, rather than feeling bitter, I tried to have a positive influence on whatever and whomever I could. I had a deep desire to provide my kids with a happy, healthy childhood. They didn't deserve to have my disappointments cast a shadow over their lives. They did not have to know I was afraid about what the future might hold. They deserved for their mom to have a smile on her face when they woke up in the morning and when they came home at the end of the day. Deep inside me, I believed I could be better for the world, and I could make a bigger difference, *because of* (not in spite of) the disappointments in my life . . . even when I didn't know how.

A couple of my favorite bible verses provided encouragement at that time. Hebrews 11:1 says, *"Now faith is being sure of what we hope for and certain of what we do not see.*"[9] And Jeremiah 29:11 says, *"For I know the plans I have for you,' declares the Lord, 'plans to prosper you and not to harm you, plans to give you hope and a future.'"*[10] I posted bible verses in various places on sticky notes. They reminded me that everything would be okay. They also reminded me that I wasn't in control of my life. I was an influencer, but not in control.

My story has a happy ending. I met my husband, Steve, ten years ago and married him in 2017. I inherited two more kids who I really enjoy, the business I've owned for over twenty years is still thriving, and the kids are all happy, successful adults. The five kids enjoy hanging out with one another. Steve makes me laugh every day. He is also golden in treating all five of our kids as if they are his own. I didn't think that would be possible. #lucky.

I'm on the other side of the desert and I feel equipped to encourage others. I would have no idea how to spark if I didn't experience all of the extinguishing muck.

Are you experiencing your own desert crossing? Are you still hanging onto a desert crossing from the past? Are you carrying it around with you? Do people see it?

You can get past your muck, but it requires work. It starts with a decision to not let life get you down. You also have to decide to what degree you want to bring others into your own difficulty. Rather than positioning to receive sympathy, find ways to become a stronger and more influential woman. Begin to imagine what your own happy ending will look like.

You can start by completing the exercise on the next page.

Let's talk about you:

1. What disappointments have you dealt with in your life?

2. What happened in your childhood that you have had difficulty letting go of or that is still adversely affecting your happiness and contentment?

3. In what ways have these disappointments shaped who you are today?

4. How have you benefitted by your disappointments?

Women I've coached over the years have shared disappointments in plenty of areas. Perhaps you can relate to some of these in your own life:

☐ I'm disappointed I didn't save more money.

☐ I'm disappointed by how much weight I've gained.

☐ I'm disappointed my adult kids are not independent.

☐ I'm disappointed my husband and I do not have things in common.

☐ I'm disappointed my kids don't visit more.

☐ I'm disappointed I do not have any hobbies or interests of my own.

☐ I'm disappointed I don't love my job.

☐ I'm disappointed I gave up my career to stay home with the kids.

☐ I'm disappointed I was unable to have kids.

☐ I'm disappointed my health is not better.

☐ I'm disappointed I didn't stay in touch with friends.

You'll notice from this list that I'm not including catastrophic disappointments. I know there are gigantic disappointments in life, some that feel almost insurmountable like serious addictions, cancer diagnoses, mental illness, and losing someone you love. But for now, let's focus on the less severe disappointments that can contribute to chronic pain or sadness in your life. Dealing with these will help prepare you for everything else life throws at you.

What can you do to deal with the disappointments you've identified? Focusing on gratitude is a concrete starting point that can contribute to a successful spark.

Gratitude is a Strategy

Most of us do our greatest growing during our most difficult times—the crucibles of life. Gratitude can play a part in a couple of ways:

You can be grateful for your growth as a person. Difficulty can play a role in helping you become a calmer, more humbler person.

- You can be grateful for becoming better-equipped to help others—eventually. Watch for silver linings to appear.

- Sometimes when we don't get what we want, we get something better. For example, maybe your first offer on a home wasn't accepted—and then you found a house you liked even better. Or it's possible you were downsized out of a job and that led you to a new job where you discovered your calling. Perhaps an unhappy marriage ended—and then you met the love of your life.

Gratitude didn't come easily for me. I've been a lot of things before grateful: upset, afraid, jealous, resentful, regretful, and disappointed. But it was worth it to embrace gratitude.

Many of the books I've read say the same thing: your life is better when it's not perfect.

Use your disappointments well. Put them to work. Reframe your thinking about them. Let them be okay. Spark anyway.

PART III
MAKE EVERYTHING BRIGHTER

SPARK NOTE!

Ignite On: Connecting

"I have often waited for my house to be in order and my life to be less 'messy' before initiating or showing up in friendship. What I am learning is that friendship works best when I show up just the way I am, in all of my mess, because, perfect doesn't exist. And 'perfect' leaves us lonely."

~ Diane Banfield

STEP SEVEN
SPARK HAPPINESS FOR OTHERS

We all have opportunities to make everyday moments magical for the people around us.

When my oldest daughter, Jaimie, was two years old, I took her to my friend Paula's house for a sleepover. I walked up to the door with Jaimie, who was bundled up in her snowsuit, hat, scarf, and mittens. She looked like a little marshmallow. For some reason she was holding her toothbrush in her hand rather than having it packed away in her bag. When Paula opened the door, she greeted us enthusiastically.

"Hi Jaimie! Oh my gosh, you have your toothbrush; that's fantastic!" Paula's enthusiasm made my day. There was nothing exciting about a toothbrush, but Paula made the moment feel so happy for Jaimie.

Sparking happiness applies to everyone....even little children.

Make Someone's Day

When I was in my tough season of my life—my desert-crossing—one day a friend got really honest with me. She said, "You are not unhappy because of what you're not getting; you're unhappy because of what you're not giving." *Ouch*.

Sometimes, it's tempting to lash out at someone who tells us something that's uncomfortable to hear. But, you know what? My friend was right. It doesn't cost a thing to make someone else's day. Even during some of our most difficult seasons, we can still spread joy. If you're looking for more happiness and more confidence, turn your attention to how your attitude can change the people and atmosphere around you. You may be short on time, but it doesn't take long to show kindness as you go through daily routines.

I was introduced to the concept of simple kindnesses a number of years ago when I read a treasure of a book called *Life As A Daymaker* by David Wagner.[11] We have dozens of opportunities every day to be a Daymaker.

Remember your above-the-line and below-the-line behaviors? In order to learn to spark, creating happiness for others and *adding deposits* to others needs to become a habit through routine practice. Whether we're talking about family members, friends, neighbors, co-workers, or even strangers, you have numerous opportunities every day to help others feel positive about you, their environments, and themselves.

I met one of my friends for coffee recently. When we were waiting for our drinks, she said to the barista, "I was in here yesterday, and you served me. I want you to know you were so nice to me, and I was having a moment where I really needed someone to be nice. So,

I want to thank you." When we sat down, my friend told me she had lost a customer relationship the day before, was feeling bad about herself, and the barista was so kind and friendly to her, it made her feel better.

It doesn't matter whether you're leading an important corporate initiative or shopping for groceries, if you are kind and you care about the impact you have on others, you will become a *woman who sparks*.

Daymaking Opportunities

Do you feel stretched thin, exhausted, and overwhelmed? Stress about what's going to happen—or *needs to* happen—in the future can rob you of opportunities to enjoy each day. I want to challenge you to spend small amounts of time making everyday moments meaningful. I think you'll like the return on your investment.

Here are a few areas where you can intentionally make someone's day:

- Smile at others. It will make everyone feel better about life—even when things are difficult and frustrating.

- Be gracious when someone makes a mistake—it's so much better than being indignant and angry. The people around you will remember when you handle a situation in a classy way.

- Be kind. This can be as simple as keeping an eye open while driving for someone who may be trying to switch lanes. You might never meet that person, but when you choose kindness, you're sparking.

- Step back. Do you notice the person behind you at the grocery store with two items? You can invite that person to go ahead of you. Look for opportunities to do the same thing at work and home.

- Notice the best. Make a point to notice the beautiful and inspiring things about other people rather than focusing on things you don't like.

- Be grateful. Thanking service providers and others you encounter everyday will help make you a daymaker. (Bonus! It will also keep you from carrying an air of entitlement.)

- Be patient. When you choose to be patient and understanding you can change the atmosphere around you.

Stand Out in a Crowd

I do a lot of professional speaking. In every crowd, close to the front, I seek out the friendly person. This is the participant who has a relaxed smile on her face and who affirmingly nods her head up and down at the perfect times. Her presence makes my experience as a speaker enjoyable. Knowing someone is really listening and eager to learn reminds me of why being at the event is important as I work to make a meaningful contribution to the lives of those attending. In every crowd there is also that person who sits through an entire event, arms crossed with a serious facial expression—almost disapproving. You can choose your expression. Make sure you stand out in a crowd for the right reasons.

Make Your Own Day

If you are going to be a person who brings positivity, kindness, and happiness to others, you need to start by bringing those same things to yourself. You need to take care of yourself so you can make a positive difference in the world.

The inventory below will give you an opportunity to think about how you feel about yourself and your habits.

Make Your Day Great

What things are you doing to make yourself feel happy, calm, and centered?
Below is a list to get you started. Put a checkmark by the things you currently do—or things you'd like to do—to make your life better. Then add your own.

- ☐ Wake up thirty minutes early and have quiet time before your family starts to wake up.
- ☐ Work out in the morning.
- ☐ Drink plenty of water during the day.
- ☐ Watch a favorite TV show with your spouse or significant other two or three times a week.
- ☐ Walk thirty minutes every day.
- ☐ Sit by the fireplace with a good book.
- ☐ Keep a gratitude journal.
- ☐ Meet a friend for dinner.
- ☐ Host a gathering.
- ☐ Keep your home neat and tidy.
- ☐ Take time to relax.

☐ Schedule a weekly date night with your spouse or significant other.

☐ _____

☐ _____

In what ways are you robbing yourself of happiness, calmness and a sense of being centered?
Below is a list to get you started. Again, add your own.

☐ I don't sleep enough.

☐ I spend too much time surfing social media.

☐ I compare myself to others.

☐ I don't drink enough water.

☐ I drink too much wine.

☐ I eat too much sugar.

☐ I have so many clothes in my closet that I'm overwhelmed.

☐ I yell at my kids every day.

☐ I don't take time to exercise.

☐ I let myself sleep too long.

☐ Magazines and newspapers are piling up around me.

☐ I drink too much coffee.

☐ I spend money foolishly.

☐ I talk about my friends behind their back.

☐ I think about what's wrong with me rather than what's right.

☐ _____

☐ _____

There is no time like now to start improving your life and the lives of those around you. Many times you can't control what's happening around you, but you can control your response. Regardless of what is going on in your world, can you remain calm, affirming, patient, gracious, forgiving, humble, and caring. Your positive, caring response will make someone's day—and it will help you create a life that sparks.

Take Action

You can also take things a step further and get strategic about being a Daymaker. What action item can you put on your calendar that will make someone's day?

I'll never forget accidentally being on-hand when my aunt, who was living in an assisted living home, received flowers I had ordered for her the day before. I had no idea how much joy they would bring. She smiled and laughed and thanked me so many times I lost count. It was a little thing that made a big impact.

I have also experienced how a kind gesture can create lasting memories. When my kids were little, I was often overwhelmed. When my twins, Ben and Steph, were born, Jaimie was two. I like things to be neat and orderly, but, as you can imagine, I didn't have time for that with all of those little people running around.

I vividly remember the kind gestures of others. My sister-in-law came over one day and announced she was there to wash my kitchen floor. I had a neighbor who came over a few times a week and swept my dining room and kitchen while we chatted. My mother-in-law picked up my husband's shirts every week to wash and iron them. Another neighbor periodically came over to pick up my two-year-old so I only had two kids in the house for a while.

Each of those people had busy lives of their own—and yet they took time to make my day easier. Sometimes minor acts of service can help create a legacy of kindness.

Daymaking sends a message to people: "I'm thinking of you. You're important to me."

Make your list. How will you make someone's day?

STEP EIGHT
Stay Calm

You probably didn't pick up this book to have someone tell you to "stay calm."

It doesn't exactly sound exciting or even "sparkly"—and yet it may be the secret ingredient that will provide you with the peace and presence to be an influential woman in any situation.

People are drawn to you when you are calm. And when you withstand the tests of everyday life patiently, you may not be creating sparks, but you will certainly prevent yourself from destroying someone else's sparks. Once again, take a moment to think about those women you know who light up a room the moment they walk in. What is it about them? Is it how they feel about themselves? Or how they make you feel about yourself? I would guess it's a combination of those two things.

My husband is an example of someone who is good at helping the people around him by remaining calm.

He doesn't get mad at other drivers, he doesn't overreact when the kids are being kids, and he doesn't overreact when we're dealing with a variety of frustrations and issues that come along with daily living. He has confidence that everything will work out. I share that perspective. As a result, we enjoy a calm environment at home. I don't have to endure negative emotion from my husband and that means his attitude allows me to maintain a positive attitude and enjoy happiness every day.

Because I tend to be calm, I am often a voice of reason for my friends. Almost all of them have teenaged and young adult children. As you can imagine, all kinds of things are going on in the lives of so many young people. I will get an occasional text, *"Hey do you have time to meet for a glass of wine?"* That is code for, *"I need you to talk me off a ledge,"* or *"I could use some advice."* They can always use reassurance to help them remain calm, to believe that everything will work out, and to know that things that are happening are predictable.

Do you feel like you can play the role of the calm voice of reason in your friends' lives?

Or are you caught up thinking about times when you've overreacted and made a situation worse?

I've had moments I look back on and cringe. There have been times when I was a daybreaker instead of a daymaker. There have been times when others were forced to endure my emotion as it negatively impacted their day.

But here's the good news: *you can learn from the past, you can ask others for forgiveness, and you can change how you deal with situations in the future.*

A Non-Yelling Family

I credit my daughter, Jaimie, with shutting down my not-very-calm nature as a young mom. One day, when she was about twelve years old (and likely pushing several of my buttons) I let her have it. As I was in a full-on, not-very-attractive yelling episode, she calmly replied, "Mom, I've decided when you yell at me, I'm not going to yell back." Huh. That was interesting to me. My first thought was "Why you little...." I'm kidding. I was impressed. I thought "If you can do that, I can do that."

We went downstairs and announced this to Ben and Steph, who were ten at the time. That day, we became a non-yelling family. I became a non-yelling mom.

Now, did this mean we never yelled? Of course not. What it did mean, though, is I tried very hard, as the mom, to model that behavior. I needed to demonstrate the value we established. And when I yelled, I apologized. I provided friendly accountability for my kids. I often said, "Hey, use your words." Rather than focusing on what *not* to do, I focused on what they *could* do instead.

Author Stephen Covey also influenced my desire to consider carefully how I relate to my kids. In *The Seven Habits of Highly Effective People*, he talked about looking into his future, of imagining his funeral, and of wanting his children to tell stories of how much he loved and understood them. He wrote, "If one of my children was about to speak, I would want his heart to be filled with pleasant memories of deep, meaningful times together. I would want him to remember me as a loving father who shared the fun and pain of growing up. I would want to have listened, and loved, and helped.

I would want him to know I wasn't perfect, but that I had tried with everything I had. And that, perhaps more than anybody in the world, I loved him." He continued, "But I don't always see those values. I get caught up in the thick of thin things, and the way I interact with my children often bears little resemblance to the way I deeply feel about them."[12]

Covey's story struck a nerve with me. As I moved forward through two decades of child-rearing, I thought about this every day: *be kind, be calm, be understanding.*

As my kids got older and started dealing with their own challenges, I began to coach them to be calm. When Jaimie was sixteen, she was having some difficulty with her cell phone. I encouraged her to call Verizon. Because this was her first call of a customer service nature, I gave her a few tips:

1. Make sure you remain calm.

2. Use your regular voice. Do not raise your voice or talk louder.

3. If they are not addressing your frustration in the way you want, continue to remain calm.

Jaimie followed those steps and, at the end of the call, she hung up and said, "Mom, he was so nice to me." She was beaming. It's easier for people to be nice when you're calm.

Unloading our emotions on someone else isn't likely to change a situation (at least not in a positive way). But we can make it easier to work through something difficult with someone by remaining calm. Think about your own experiences. Are you more productive, and do you feel better, when you're in a calm, rational conversation with someone or when they are, to use my kids' phrase, freaking out?

When Ben and Steph were about twelve, I was driving them home from school. Each of them had a friend along. Somehow the twins got into a full-blown fight with one another. I pulled over to the side of the road, turned around, and calmly said, "Hey you two. You can calm down right now, and we'll continue. Or you can continue with this fighting, and I'll turn around and take your friends home." Yep, I really said that. Calmly. Thank you, Jaimie. As I began to drive, I heard Ben's friend say to him, "You're lucky your mom doesn't yell at you, because my mom yells at me all the time." Listen, I've been that mom. And like I've said more than once, I credit my wise twelve-year old daughter for setting me straight on that point.

It's important that you also understand I still struggled. I put a stake in the ground, declared myself a calm, non-yelling person. And, I still yelled. Not a lot, but when I did, it was not pretty. I owned it, though. If you asked my kids how many times I yelled at them after the day we became a non-yelling family, they all know the answer. Three. Three extremely loud times. And they would also laugh. The reason they would laugh is because I looked and sounded completely ridiculous. Ugh.

There are times when you will struggle to remain calm too. But what's important is that you decide what you need to do about your emotional outbursts, own it when you mess up, and make progress in the long run.

Letting Go

Do you struggle to remain calm because it feels like relaxing will cause everything to fall apart? If you feel a need to control the things happening around you, it's difficult to remain calm. The more you need to ensure things go as they should, the more you will impose yourself. And the more you impose yourself, the less calm you will be able to be.

If you struggle with being a controlling person, it may be difficult to recognize—after all, you feel like you're only doing what essential.

However, you likely recognize when others struggle with being a controlling person.

Here's a list of common characteristics of controlling people:

- They want to be in charge of planning to make sure it's "done *right*."

- They are in the middle of every project, to ensure the work is done the way they would do it.

- They coordinate the details that involve them and others, again to ensure they're taken care of in one right way.

- They hover over others while they are working to make sure the job is done right.

- They correct the manner in which people do things: how the towels are folded, how the dishwasher is loaded, and how the bed is made, for instance.

- They have a tendency to do things themselves so they are done right.

- If they overhear others talking, they may regularly chime in with, "Hey what are you guys talking about?"

- They like to be aware of the details related to everything.

Is this you? If so . . . aren't you exhausted?

If you are a controlling person, you can practice calming down by letting go of situations and letting other people use their own methods. Relax. Things can be okay without you at the front and center. At work, trust that others know what they're doing and refrain from needing to know everything. As your friends are settling up a dinner bill, your family is making plans for the holiday gift exchange, or as you are with a group of people packing a cooler for a concert and a picnic, sit back a bit and let the others who are involved take the lead role. See what happens. I am going to guess that everything will be okay. I am not suggesting you become an uninvolved person when your group needs your involvement. I'm merely challenging your idea that it's up to you to save the day *every time*.

Five Ways to Calm Down:

1. **Manage your emotions.** Talk in a conversational tone of voice. Expressing your emotions loudly won't change the situation. You will get better results if you leave your emotions off the table.

2. **Don't yell.** I know this one is related to #1, but it is important enough to stand alone. This may pertain primarily to women with children. So many moms yell at their kids. This is something to think about.

3. **Let others handle the details.** The notion of handling things so they're done *right*? Well, it's kind of a self-centered view. There are so many ways to do things. You'll see if you step back, everything will be okay. You can practice. If someone says, "How do you want me to do this?" Your reply can be, "However you'd like." It may not be how you would slice the limes or cut the tomatoes or fold the towels. Can that be okay? Let me rephrase because it's not really a question: That can be okay.

4. **Have regard for others' disappointments.** You may have noticed that, when other people are disappointed, they become emotional. They may yell, pout, sulk, ignore you, and say things that are uncomfortable. Keep in mind: their disappointment is not about you, it's about them. Their reaction is also not about you, it's about them. Regardless of how they respond, you do not have to respond in kind. You can issue a simple acknowledgment. "I'm sorry for how this is affecting you."

5. **Keep things in perspective.** I can't underscore this enough. Life is imperfect, people are imperfect, and situations are imperfect. So often, things will not go as you would like. Expect that. Expect the imperfect. I love Brené Brown's advice in her book, *Brave the Wilderness*. She says, "Embrace the suck."[13]

PART IV
DISCOVER YOUR BIGGER PURPOSE

SPARK NOTE!
Ignite On: Focus

"Be mindful of your thoughts. Positive thoughts! And be aware when they turn negative so you can turn them around."

~ Rikki Meister

STEP NINE
DISCOVER YOUR PURPOSE AND PASSION

Chances are there's something stirring inside of you—and you need to figure out what it is.

Why did you pick up this book in the first place? It's possible you know you were made to be and do more than your current life reflects. At this point you may feel hopeful about the future—or you might be discouraged, feeling like life is passing you by and you'll never make a difference.

Here's the good news: you might already be farther along than you think. Finding your purpose in life is a culmination of hundreds or even thousands of small moments. They are like seeds planted in our lives.

If we listen, ponder, pay attention, and even look for signs, we may find something with the potential to grow into a meaningful part of our lives. The signs may be small and fleeting. Perhaps it will be a passing thought of your own, a passing comment by a friend, or something in an article that resonates with you. It might come in the form of a sentence spoken by the pastor of your church, a discussion during your performance review at work, a special talent you exhibit, or a habit that takes hold in your life.

These seeds can give you insights into your strengths, your passions, and your sources of happiness. They can help you understand who you are and what you are intended to accomplish in the world. Signs can help you know what you like and what you don't like. They can help you pick your friends or leave a job. The problem for most of us is that we're not paying attention.

As I think about the seeds and signs that I've encountered in my life, I recognize that I've always been drawn to books. (You may have noticed!) I like being alone with my thoughts. I am happiest when I am filling my head with ideas and information. With each book I read, I underline, write notes in the margins, dog ear the pages, fill up the inside covers with my scribblings, and journal the best nuggets in notebooks. Book by book, my interest in writing my own began to take hold.

A Seed Toward Purpose

In 2005, I received a gift from my dear friend and business partner, Nancy. She gave me a copy of *Pathway to Purpose for Women,* by Katie Brazelton.[14] On the heels of my two divorces, and knee deep in a funk, it was exactly what I needed. I couldn't put that book down. Katie's words jumped off the pages at me. Every word inspired me. She was so authentic, willing to share her struggles, her anguish, the messiness of her life, and her journey to discover her big purpose in life. I think

I underlined every sentence in her book. She struck me as an amazing, talented, beautiful, and funny woman whose life was imperfect, yet so perfect. I wanted to be her. At the back of the book was a page, "How to Contact the Author." I could email her, I could hire her to speak, or I could reach out for a Life Plan referral. It was obvious: God wanted me to go to California to meet with Katie. She was, after all, an encourager of women. And I needed encouragement.

I sent an email to Katie and said, *"I have to meet you."* She responded immediately, we exchanged a series of emails to sort out the details, and off I went a month later to create a life plan. My problems would soon be over. I headed to California where I spent two days working hard under Katie's direction. I surrendered my guilt and regret into the ocean at Laguna Beach, reflected on my life (past, present and future), and explored my passions.

It was a life changing experience.

Katie helped set me on a course that would guide me for the rest of my life. And she did it without changing who I was. Instead, she helped me discover the seeds in my life that needed care so they could grow into something meaningful.

Time to Grow

After several hours of work, we sorted through pages of notes and listed my top five passions:

1. I have a heart for women.

2. I want to be a blessing to others.

3. I want to leverage my life experiences to help others deal with theirs.

4. I love to work.

5. I love to speak and write.

Katie then helped me summarize these five passions into my purpose. My purpose in life is to *Be an encourager of women as a writer, speaker, and coach.* So, there it was in March 2006. I put a stake in the ground. I decided the first thing I would do is write a book.

Katie told me, "When you write your book, I will write your foreword." I have chills. I'm beyond excited that she wrote my foreword. If you didn't read it, please go back and read it!

Did you notice, however, that it's been a while since 2006? I soon learned how difficult it is to get unstuck. I didn't immediately start writing a book. Instead, I simply spent several years throwing notes in a box.

It was difficult to go in a new direction when I was in the middle of a full life already. Years ago, I had started to think of my life as a timeline, sectioned off in decades. You know as well as I do, we can't do everything all at once. I knew I would have time down the road for a new adventure. At the time, I was forty-three and I had three kids who were heading off to college soon. I had to get through that season with things I already had in place. But all the while the passion and purpose for this book were percolating inside me.

Sometimes it will take years for a seed of a dream to grow and flourish in your life. What's important is to make sure you keep tending and caring for it.

Discover Your Purpose and Passion

If you feel disenchanted with how your life has turned out so far, it's a sign you need to dig deeper. Don't settle for *good enough*. Don't settle for *comfortable*. I've heard plenty of women say, "Things are fine." Fine? Is that enough? If things are fine for you, are you inspired? Are you inspiring others? Are you excited?

Don't allow yourself to live a mediocre life, to be bored, and to flip through channels on your life's remote control. Demand more of yourself than that.

Is there a dream you need to be chasing? Your purpose in life probably won't look at all like mine, but it does need to be that one thing you know is worth getting up and chasing after every morning.

If it's not clear, take time to slow down and look at your life carefully. It's possible seeds have already been planted—and what they are will become clear when you get serious about figuring out why you're here and how you can make a difference in the world.

Pay attention to significant experiences, things you are good at, and challenges you've struggled to overcome. If you look closely enough, you will find the things that will make a difference for you—and they might even change the trajectory of your life and the lives of people around you. Perhaps you will discover your own path to embrace contentment, a shift in how you approach your role, or a breakthrough in your relationship with a spouse. You may discover a way to drastically improve your health. It's also possible you'll find new inspiration in your work or in a hobby.

Use the worksheet on the next page to start looking for how one of these things may help reveal your passion and purpose.

Time to reflect

1. What brings you joy? What lights you up?

2. If you could do anything with your time, what are the things you would choose to do?

3. Who is doing something that you would love to do? What is she doing?

4. What are some of the seeds planted in your life over the years?

STEP TEN
DO IT AFRAID

Are negative voices playing in the back of your head and drowning out your passion for life?

Is fear threatening to destroy your dreams and keeping you from becoming the person you were meant to be? In order to fulfill your purpose, and become a *woman who sparks*, you need to govern your fear.

Don't get me wrong, fear has a place in our lives. We need to identify and manage risk. But we also need to keep fear in perspective, or it *will* get in the way.

Are you stuck in an uninspiring job because you're afraid to move on? Do you have a vision for the future, but you're afraid of what other people would think if you shared it? The truth is that you might have to carefully orchestrate a career move and people might think your big dream is crazy. But the bigger question is whether you can afford to miss out on what might be possible if you're willing to take some big, bold, carefully calculated risks.

I have times when fear seeps in. Every time I watch a YouTube video, listen to a podcast, or read a book, I pause and wonder if I can bring the same level of value as those that inspire me. At the same time, I'm not willing to waste a possible chance of a lifetime. I want to be fully used up when I die. In order to do that, I'm willing to do life . . . a little bit afraid.

Will you join me?

Gaining Perspective

Fear is inconsistent. At this moment, you are likely confident about some things in your life and insecure in other areas. Over time, you may have seasons of life where you're filled with confidence. Then suddenly something will happen that almost destroys your confidence and you're suddenly filled with self-doubt. Fear has a way of sneaking up on you and messing with your head.

I remember talking to a young woman about a decision she had to make regarding a school change. She was miserable in her situation, but she was also paralyzed with fear by the thought of making a change.

We discussed her problem for a long time. Finally, she said, *"What if it's worse?"*

I immediately asked, *"What if it's better?"*

It turns out this is a thought that had not crossed her mind. It surprised her, and it helped ease her fear. She ultimately decided to change schools. She did it afraid. And, the outcome was perfect.

What about you? What are you afraid of?

- Looking for a new, more fulfilling job?
- Having a difficult conversation with your spouse?
- Giving a presentation at work?
- Moving toward a dream?
- Not having enough money?
- Asking for a raise?
- Moving to a new city?
- Leaving an unfulfilling relationship?
- Cutting your hair short?
- Launching a new business?

Do you have an internal voice that is not helping?

- *You'll never find a better job.*
- *This is not your spouse's problem—it's yours.*
- *No one will want to hire you.*
- *You will never succeed in a new venture.*
- *You cannot make your dream come true like that other person has.*
- *You'll not meet someone else.*
- *You will be alone if you leave.*
- *You've always had long hair; you should stay with what you know.*
- *You're not worth more money.*
- *A business? Who are you kidding?*

Does any of this sound familiar? Do you have self-talk trying to rob you of your confidence?

We are all more alike than we are different. We are all trying to do the best we can in life yet not sure we're good enough. Even if we feel like we're good enough, there is still the fear that we are not *as* "good enough" as the person next to us or as another person doing the same thing.

As we discussed earlier, confidence is not about your ability to do something—confidence is about your ability to figure it out. Think back over your life. Have you been in difficult situations? Most of us have. Have you been able to figure out a solution? I am going to guess that you likely have. You're still here. You're reading this book. You're on a journey of some kind. Along the way, you have figured things out. Do you have confidence that your journey will continue?

Sometimes we have to deal with the unpleasant stuff that comes our way. And, often, we have to get rid of this stuff before we can focus on the good stuff. You may be thinking, "*I can't think about my dreams and passions, because I have all of these problems in my life.*" You might be struggling with financial difficulties, illness, poor relationships, self-doubt, or fear of a new situation. Let's talk about this below-the-line stuff first, this negative stuff. Then we'll talk about the fun stuff—the new dreams and passions, that land above the line.

It's difficult to thrive when we're in the throes of surviving. I know what that's like. When my second marriage ended, I was filled with self-doubt, insecurity, and fear. The worrying kept me awake at night. My mind would not shut off. I would lie in bed thinking about worst-case scenarios: *I'll have to work until I die. I won't be able to help my kids with college. I will lose our*

house. I will wear my current wardrobe for the next decade.
I am wrecking my kids' lives....

When the early hours of the morning arrived, as I lay there ruminating on awful thoughts, I would hear the paper being delivered on my doorstep.

Thump.

I *hated* hearing that newspaper arrive. It meant another sleepless night had passed. The emotional and physical exhaustion lasted for months.

Then, one day I didn't hear it. I didn't wake up at 4:00 am. I didn't lie in bed worrying. I was *finally* able to sleep. Gradually, my financial situation improved; my debt started to decrease, and my income started to increase. I cleaned up more things and the situation got better. It took several *years* to feel safe and comfortable again. But eventually it all worked out. I helped my kids with college, kept the house, my wardrobe was fine, and . . . well . . . I probably will work until I die—but only because I want to. Best of all, today I live with a lot less fear.

I am confident that those were the worst of my years.

What are you trying to survive? Have you encountered any of these challenging situations?

☐ I have to pay for my own college.

☐ I have to save for retirement.

☐ I lost my job.

☐ I am going through an unwanted divorce.

☐ I have to take on a new responsibility at work.

☐ I've been given a big project.

☐ The roof is leaking.

☐ I haven't met my life partner.

☐ I am battling an illness.

☐ I have an unexpected car repair bill.

☐ I have too much on my plate.

☐ I'm starting a new job.

☐ I'm in a bad relationship.

☐ I don't have energy.

☐ I've gained ten pounds (or more).

How many of these situations have you encountered in your life? Did you figure it out? Did you resolve it? If it couldn't be resolved, did you learn to accept it? Do you have any reason to suggest you will not be able to figure out more situations that emerge in your future?

The solution to fear is confidence. Confidence is the ability to figure things out. *"I am confident I'll be able to figure out the things*

> **"Confidence is the ability to figure things out."**

that come my way, because— up to this point—I've been able to do that." If you can figure things out, the fear will dissipate.

If something feels too overwhelming, focus on the first step. That is all you have to do.

- If you want to lose ten pounds, you could decide to not eat after 7:00 P.M. or give up your regular soda. Choose one thing. Then add the next and the next.

- If your roof is leaking, take the first step: reach out to your friends for the name of a roofer. Get an estimate.

- If you're starting a new job, focus on getting through your first day.

- If you need to save more for retirement, start educating yourself by reading some articles on the Internet.

You can experience success—and defeat fear—one small step at a time.

Own Your Value

As I shared earlier, your confidence to survive and solve situations will be stronger if you believe in your worth. You need to hold your head high and say, *"My worth as a person is equal to that of others."* You have the exact same right as every person around you to overcome challenges and pursue your dreams. You have the same right to be happy and to build a meaningful life.

> "Did you know self-esteem is a subjective evaluation of your self-worth? What we're talking about is your own attitude about your value as a person — and it might need to change."

If you have low self-esteem, it is likely that an accumulation of events in your life have led you to think less of yourself. The damage may have started in your childhood. Perhaps your parents were not affectionate. They might not have openly expressed their love, encouraged you, or told you that you were amazing. Maybe you were not a good athlete and didn't make the team. Maybe you got left out of activities with friends—or didn't have friends. As an adult, perhaps you did not get hired for a job that really mattered to you. Or a special boyfriend broke up with you. With these kinds of experiences, along with the effects on our confidence, it's no wonder many women become fearful.

If you struggle with low self-esteem and self-doubt, it's okay. What is not okay, however, is allowing it to paralyze you. I don't want to over-simplify a difficult and maybe sad reality for you. I know many people grapple with self-esteem and self-doubt issues in life, even those who are extremely successful in life. Rather than trying to avoid dealing with those emotions, you can start focusing on what you can do.

Low self-esteem is tied to an internal belief that "I am not worthy." But I have news: ***You.Are.Worthy***.

Self-doubt is tied to your belief that you cannot do something. You *can*. *You can do whatever you set your mind to.* You will probably have to do it afraid.

Some Ways To Overcome Fear:

1. **Do your research.** Learn, learn, learn. I told you that I have experienced some fear and self-doubt related to this book. I'm a research geek. I love to tackle problems by reading articles and books, listening to podcasts, and watching YouTube videos. I've come across so much helpful advice about writing a book and launching this kind of business. And, even more helpful, I've been able to read the stories of others' self-doubt as they launched their businesses or wrote their first books. Misery loves company. The stories of fear, doubt, and even failure

are the stories that have helped me the most. Get yourself some Brené Brown.[15] She has spent the last twenty years researching vulnerability and shame. Her books are a must read if you're struggling with your own self-worth.

2. **Try new things:** Your confidence will increase as you try new things and prove to yourself that you can be successful. Recently, my daughter Steph made a pie from scratch, including the pie crust. Have you ever thought, "I could never make a pie? Who makes pies in this day and age?" Steph had that passing thought. I asked her what inspired her to make a pie? She said, "Well, I went to the apple orchard today to get apples, and I wanted to see if I could do it." She did it. She figured it out. And it was easier than she imagined it would be.

3. **Keep your social media surfing in its proper perspective:** As I mentioned earlier, everyone on Facebook and Instagram looks so happy. And beautiful. It's easy to believe they are always this happy. Don't believe that for a moment. Most of the happy, smiling, beautiful people whose pictures you are looking at with envy have their own struggles. Their struggles may not be yours, but they have them. While you are envying their posts, they may be envying yours.

4. **Manage Your Self-Talk:** We've already talked about self-talk as a way to cultivate confidence. But this is such a trap for so many of us that we're going to talk about it again. Fear will gain momentum if you get stuck in your head. *"I'm afraid she doesn't like me," "I'm afraid I don't fit in." "I'm afraid they're talking about me."*

People are less focused on you than you may think. Years ago, I went on a weekend trip with two girl-friends. While one was at the register making a purchase, the other two of us were off to the side chatting and laughing. As we proceeded from the store, our friend was quiet. I asked if something was troubling her, and she said, *"I know you guys were laughing at me about something."* This was not true at all. Our conversation had nothing to do with her. But it's also the kind of self-talk that could ensnare any one of us. In reality, people have their own interests, worries, and thoughts that they are consumed with (as well as their own moments of laughter). They are less consumed with you than you think.

5. **Incorporate positive affirmations into your life:** Another way to combat self-talk is by using positive affirmations. When you catch yourself saying something like, "I'm afraid I can't do it" or "things will never get better" find something to replace those thoughts. You can "get out of your head" by saying affirmations out loud or writing them down. You may want to write these on some sticky notes or notecards, then put them where they are visible. Select a couple that resonate with you from the list below.

- I am grateful for my life.
- I am excited about the passions and purpose I am dreaming about now.
- I can achieve whatever I set out to achieve.
- I can figure it out.
- It won't always be like this.
- I am a good person.
- I may be sad right now, but I'll be happy again. I just need some time.

- It's okay if some bad things co-exist with the good things I have.
- I am not alone in my struggles.
- I can take one step today toward my dream.
- Life is not perfect.
- No one owes me anything.
- I can be a Daymaker.

6. **BREATHE:** When you're feeling afraid, anxious, or maybe even panicky, STOP. Focus on your breathing. Count to five as you inhale. Then exhale as you count to nine. Repeat this several times. Then ask yourself, "Am I okay right now?"

As you go through your life, you will have challenging things to deal with. Some of these are below-the-line situations that add negativity to your life. Believe in yourself. You can deal with them to get yourself back up to neutral. And then, you can harness your dreams, passions, interests, and choices to add positivity to your life.

Take the first step and believe in your ability to move your dreams forward.

Spark Note!

Ignite On: Caring For Yourself

"I once heard, 'if you don't take care of yourself, you won't be able to take care of others.' It's a reminder as a mom, wife, daughter, sister, that YOU are the most important person in your life."

~ Shelly Banach Gebert

STEP ELEVEN
GO GET YOUR SPARKS!

Can you imagine what it would be like to live out your dream, passion, and purpose in life on a daily basis?

All the work you've done so far has created a foundation on which to build your future life.

In this book you have:

- Thought about yourself.

- Looked at your past.

- Assessed your current situation.

- Considered happiness, confidence, daymaking, and calmness.

- Remembered your disappointments.

- Pondered your purpose and passions.

- Reflected on fear.

Now it's time for you to bring it all together and go get your sparks! What can you do to bring more happiness to your days? How can you feel more confident? How can you create a better future for yourself? How can you make sure you're not squandering your life away? What do you need to do to be able to spark?

Too many women squash their own dreams, because they become overwhelmed with the *how*.

- "How would I ever do that?"
- "I don't have the skills or talent to do this."
- "I don't have time to do another thing."

That type of thinking is often accompanied by self-doubt.

- "I could never do that—it's for other people."
- "How will I ever make this better?"

As a result of these questions, many women never strategize to improve, write down the dream, and experience living with passion and purpose.

Don't let doubt hold you back. You *can* do this. You can find the time to do the things that matter most to you. Your life can become better. You can figure things out. Your dreams can come true. This chapter will show you how.

Facing Life Challenges

If you're like most women, you probably feel like you are being pulled in a gazillion directions and there are not enough hours in a day. If you don't have a plan to prioritize all the things clamoring for your attention, it's likely you collapse into bed at the end of the day not feeling good about *anything*.

I want to help you do the soul-satisfying work of really digging in. You can't do everything at once, but you can start somewhere. You can identify one thing. Or two. Maybe even three.

Let's build a plan together.

Make Planning Your First Priority

If you're thinking, *"For heaven sakes, Aleta, if you think I have time for some kind of list-making exercise or big plan, you're crazy."*

I understand. Let's imagine you don't delve in and do the work. After all, you're right. You don't have time for all of the things already on your to-do list, let alone for this. I get it. Let's stop and think about this for a moment:

- What's at risk for you if you don't do the work? What if you don't stop, think, and plan?

- Would you take a trip without doing the research and creating an itinerary?

- Would you launch a business without a plan?

- Would you host your daughter's wedding without making lists and prioritizing all the elements putting pressure on your budget?

As I mentioned earlier, most people spend more time planning activities and events in their life than they spend planning their entire life—or even the day that is in front of them. However, taking time to figure out where you're going is essential to living a life that sparks.

After all, if you don't have a plan it's likely you will feel unhappy, lack confidence, and struggle to discover or live your purpose. Ultimately, a lack of planning will make it difficult, if not impossible, to live an amazing life.

Operations and Special Projects

I want you to think about your life as having two core compartments: operations and special projects.

All of the things you do every day to keep things afloat and to address the multiple areas of your life represent the operations side of your life. This includes taking care of your home, fitting in a few workouts each week, juggling your kid-related responsibilities, going to work, spending time with friends, cleaning your house, and enjoying date nights with your spouse.

> "All of the things you do every day to keep things afloat and to address the multiple areas of your life represent the operations side of your life."

The special projects are the big things: chasing a dream, trying to define your purpose, taking action on a newly discovered passion, starting a business, or transforming yourself.

> "The special projects are the big things."

Have you had experience juggling multiple things at a job? When you go to work, you have responsibilities related to your role. These are the things that are required of you each day, each week and each month. People rely on you to complete your work so they can complete their work. While taking care of all of these responsibilities, you may also be asked to work on a special project team to advance something big, something new. Perhaps it's the implementation of a new system, creating a new hiring process, overseeing the purchase of a new building, or strengthening employee engagement.

One thing I know for sure: when you are responsible for all of these things at work, it is not easy. Every day, I see women struggle to do their jobs . . . while also managing special projects.

Your life is no different. You owe it to yourself to make sure you experience happiness and satisfaction as much as possible on the operations side of your life. And, to be on fire, you have to have a dream, passion, or purpose to discover and pursue—your special project. Without both, you are not living up to your full potential. And if you are not doing that, you're shortchanging yourself—and the rest of us.

Your Operations Plan

Let's start with the operations side of your life. Where do you want to improve? You have ten areas of your life to consider. Look at the list on the next page (you may recognize it from reviewing your year-in-the-life) and choose a couple of areas that you feel most excited about taking to the next level. Feel free to refer back to your assessment of these items completed in step three. During that step, you had the opportunity to reflect on what is going well and what is not going as well as you would like.

Now it's time to get to work on making things the best they can be. What will you focus on first?

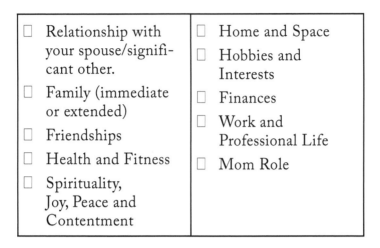

☐ Relationship with your spouse/significant other.	☐ Home and Space
	☐ Hobbies and Interests
☐ Family (immediate or extended)	☐ Finances
☐ Friendships	☐ Work and Professional Life
☐ Health and Fitness	☐ Mom Role
☐ Spirituality, Joy, Peace and Contentment	

What do you want more of? What one or two areas, if they got better, would improve the quality of your life? What feels most important to you?

Write down your answers and ideas to these questions and the additional ones that come to mind as you work. Get your journal out and start processing your thoughts.

You deserve to establish some resolutions. We don't have to think about these as New Year's Resolutions. After all, we want them to last for more than the one month after which an average 80% of New Year's Resolutions are broken. You can choose to change your life at any time. Happiness comes from making progress. It increases when you're working toward something better than you have right now.

Let's look at a couple of examples. I am going to focus on finances and health & fitness in these examples—two areas where many women are struggling.

As you begin to do your own planning, you can decide how you want to think about and document your thoughts. Do whatever works best for you. I have provided a framework below that you are welcome to use as you set your own resolutions. My Operations Improvement framework includes: Priority, Goals, Considerations, and Conclusions.

Operations Improvement Examples

Priority: *My finances*
Goals: Pay off a $6,000 credit card balance and increase the money I am putting in my 401K by one percent.
Considerations:

- How much money I can pay toward this credit card bill each month? In my current circumstances: $200

- Can I give anything up to have even more money to direct toward this credit card? Coffee shop coffee: $80 more per month

- Can I generate revenue in another way to have even more money to put toward this goal? Not at this time.

- Can I increase my 401K withholding by 1%? Yes. This will equal $1000 per year.

Conclusions:

- I will be able to pay $280 per month toward this credit card. I will have this credit card paid off in just under two years.

- By saving $1,000 more per year, I will have $25,000 - $30,000 more when I retire in 20 years. I will increase the percentage of my 401K contribution by 2% more when I have my credit card debt paid off.

In this illustration, this woman has decided to pay off debt and increase investing at the same time. If you ever find yourself in the midst of planning a resolution and feel stuck (i.e "I can't save until I have my debt paid off."), that is a good time to talk with others to gather opinions. Sometimes the best solutions are counterintuitive.

Let's look at another example:

Priority: *My Health & Fitness*
Goals: Start working out regularly and lose ten pounds.
Considerations:

- How many times a week do I want to work out and for how long? Three times for 30 minutes.

- Where would I like to work out? The gym.

- What time should I work out? 6:00 am

- Which days? Monday, Wednesday and Saturday

- How can I set myself up for success? Set out my workout clothes the night before; ask a friend to join me.

- What are some things I can do to decrease calories for weight loss:

   - Stop eating after 7:00 pm

   - Avoid the 5 C's: crackers, cookies, cake, candy and chips

   - Never eat more than one piece of bread at a restaurant

Conclusion:

- Working out three times a week feels manageable.

- By making some of the changes in my eating habits, I may be able to lose up to one pound a week.

Don't let feeling overwhelmed get in your way. You may have more things you'd like to see improve. It would be fair to say that almost all of us experience some level of dissatisfaction, or at least a longing for "better," in every area of our life. However, we don't have to fix everything to increase our levels of happiness, confidence, and fulfillment.

About eighteen months ago, I made a commitment to work out at least four times a week for thirty minutes. I've done fairly well with this goal and I'm much happier every day by simply feeling more satisfied with my amount of exercise and movement. Like you, I have many other things I'd like to give attention to, but this one thing has made a difference.

When you accomplish things (or even one thing), you begin to formulate habits. Begin with the first two areas you identified, and then you can move on to tackle new areas.

Your Special Project — Purpose and Passion

Time to get to the big stuff. As I mentioned earlier, your greatest happiness and confidence in life may come from having something to pursue. In fact, the pursuit might even be more important to you than the accomplishment itself.

Remember times in the past when you've pursued something? Once you achieved it, the feeling of accomplishment, or the newness of that thing, eventually wore off. Within a certain period of time, you may become restless for the next thing.

As you've been reading this book, you have had a number of prompts to think about what fires you up. These are the seeds that nudge you along the way, the moments that capture your attention, and the things you're noticing about what others are doing that interest you. Eventually they may become the ideas that keep you up at night.

While you continue to focus on the effectiveness of your life's operations, you also need to think about your contribution to others. What is your purpose? What are you here on this earth to do? Who are you designed to impact? Whose life can you affect in a positive way? Who inspires you? What has been whispering to you for years?

Women on Fire

- My sister, Sherri, used to tag along to work with our dad when she was a little girl. He owned a construction company and spent a lot of time in the wood shop. She loved playing alongside dad as he worked and especially loved the smell of sawdust. Throughout her life, the notion of working with wood tugged at her heart until one day she decided to take on a small project to test things out. She made a lantern out of pallet wood, inspired by a photo on Pinterest. That went well, and her next project was a coffee table. From there, she fell in love. Every year, she

makes this hobby bigger and bigger. She is always thinking about what she can add to her collection of offerings. She is absolutely obsessed. Her two-car garage has become her wood shop. She receives a steady stream of requests for custom furniture, shelving, and other wood-related items. She brings joy to others through her passion for woodworking. And the best part? She gets to smell sawdust every day!

- My friend, Jamy, discovered her passion for leading a collective giving organization when a friend came to her with the idea a few years ago. She, along with four other women, started a chapter of Impact100 in Milwaukee, Wisconsin. She never stops thinking about ways to attract even more women so the organization can grant even more money to make a difference in the lives of more people. She is on fire about this.

- I know numerous women who have left their corporate jobs to begin a coaching practice. Their purpose is to impact the lives of women and they are more on fire than they've ever been. In many situations, this is the blend of loving what they do combined with the challenge of running their own businesses.

- I met a new friend recently who is a hospice nurse. She said she is happier than she's ever been. Her exact words, "I was born to do this." She discovered her passion for serving in this area when she was fifty years old.

- I have seen many people leave high-paid corporate jobs to lead non-profits or to become missionaries. They are lit up by the opportunity to make a difference in the lives of people who are less fortunate.

- Another friend of mine made the leap from corporate America into her own business a year ago. She is making less money but is so much happier to be chasing her dream. "Scared, but happy" is the way she describes her journey!

Perhaps the work you do right now fulfills your purpose. You are making a difference in the world in exactly the way you should be. If this is true for you, then keep it up!

Or perhaps, as a mom, your big purpose is to raise independent, kind, other-centered children—and send them off into the world as positive contributors. That is fantastic. You get to decide what fires you up. No one else gets to make that decision for you. As you near your post child-raising years, you can begin to think about your next pursuit. (Get ahead of that one. I've seen a lot of women struggle when the kids leave. I've also seen a number of women handle it well because they began to strategize a couple of years prior to the nest becoming empty.)

If you have not discovered a purpose or passion, know that you deserve to do so. You deserve to discover what you can be excited about. I want you to be so excited that it's hard for you to go to sleep at the end of the day—and I want you so fired up you're ready to leap out of bed in the morning.

When you discover your true purpose in life, you will wake up every day striving to make your impact even bigger than the day before. You will live in a continual state of pursuit.

Do whatever you need to do so that you are fully used up when your time on this earth comes to an end. Don't leave anything on the table. Don't rob the world of your contribution.

During Step Nine: *Discover Your Purpose and Passion,* you answered some questions about what brings you joy. What would you do if you could do anything with your time? What do you admire in others? What has been whispering to you?

Are you ready to tackle your special project? What is it? Or, perhaps you've already started pursuing a meaningful purpose or passion. Are you ready to take it to another level?

1. On the "operations" side of your life, which one or two areas do you want to focus on?

2. What purpose or passion would you like to advance?

As we get ready to move onto Step Twelve, *Keep Your Sparks Alive,* I encourage you to get a solid grip on what you want to pursue at this point in your life. Having a plan, passion, and vision for the future will make a huge difference in your life.

Spark Note!

Ignite On: Attitude

"I tell people all the time that we can choose to be happy. When people ask me why I am so happy I say, "I woke up breathing, so it must mean it's a great day.'"

~ Beverly Valentine

STEP TWELVE
KEEP YOUR SPARKS ALIVE

A life you find fulfilling should be one brimming with happiness, confidence and purpose.

This life that sparks shouldn't be a constant struggle. In this chapter we're going to discuss ways you can build on the plans created in the last chapter to make sure you keep those dreams and passions alive.

I know you haven't worked this hard to bring your dreams alive to let them fade away quickly, but there are some things you need to build into your life so you can safeguard against losing focus.

As I said earlier, I don't want you to get tangled up in the idea of New Year's Resolutions. I do, however, want to make sure you are resolving to do better, regardless of the time of year. Your life has greater potential than you are experiencing. I know it. You are near the end of this book, and I sure hope you are swimming in your own ideas for an even better life. So, now what? How can you ensure that you will see this through?

How Will You Take Responsibility To Make Your Life Amazing?

Let's assume you are focusing on a couple of the ten areas of life we've been looking at, as well as the bigger purpose and passion part of your life. You will increase your likelihood for success, along with the degree of your success, if you are intentional. I encourage you to make every step of your journey more purposeful.

Take on one idea or commitment at a time and run it through the following seven-step process. When you take this methodical approach, I'm positive you'll nail it.

1. START WITH SMALL STEPS

Whatever you choose to focus on, make sure you are being realistic.

- If you want to lose weight, don't focus on fifty pounds, focus on your first five.

- If you want to remodel your house, choose your first room.

- If you want to work out more, don't go from zero to seven days a week; start with three. Also, don't start with an hour (maybe start with thirty minutes).

- If you want to eat better, start by cutting out one thing you love, not all of them.

- If your marriage is struggling, ask your spouse what one thing would make the biggest difference—and then focus on that one thing.

- If you want to find a new job, start by looking at what is posted online, or get your resume updated.

- If you want to create a new friend group, start by talking to a few women you know and outlining your expectations for the level of commitment needed. Women, by the way, love this invitation.

2. WRITE IN A JOURNAL

For all of the above, your first small step might be to write down your ideas. If you are working on improving areas of your life, a journal is a must. You will be using this a lot (I hope), so make sure you feel inspired by it. Shop around a bit. Find a journal that you love. And, for some of you, that may be a journal you keep on your computer, though there are benefits to the tactile reality of old-fashioned paper. Regardless of what you've identified to work on, your first step will be to brainstorm. Every area of life you are going to focus on needs its own page or more in your journal to jot down your initial ideas.

You will feel overwhelmed when you allow an entire melting pot of ideas, wishes, dreams, to-dos, fears, disappointments, self-doubt, plans, problems, and strategies to get stuck whirling around in your head.

Shift all of those thoughts from your brain to a journal. Get it out. You may even begin by creating title pages for yourself for the initial cleanse of ideas or brainstorming:

- My current fears.

- My current to-do list.

- The things that are overwhelming me right now.

- The things I want to do before the end of the year.

- The areas of my life I want to improve over the next 12 months.

- My dreams.

- What do I want my life to look like ten years from now?

- The things that fire me up.

Create your own categories. The ones mentioned above are only a starting point.

When you undertake an exercise like this, you don't think so much as you simply write. This is a stream of consciousness exercise. You already have the answers to all of these questions and more. You want them to spill out of your mind and all onto these journal pages through your pen (or fingers, as it were).

Let your journal own all of these ideas until you return again to do more thinking, planning, and strategizing.

3. CREATE HABITS

Most of the things you want to accomplish in life will fall short unless you build an infrastructure for success. Habits are something you weave into your life so that you will be better prepared to accomplish your wishes and goals.

You may have some work to do when it comes to establishing good habits. That's okay—almost all of us need to work on this.

Let's keep it simple by using a four-step process:

- Step One: Assess the habits you have. Look at each habit critically. Does it help you or hurt you?

- Step Two: Decide which habits you would like to eliminate from your life, based on your goals.

- Step Three: Decide what habits you would like to incorporate into your routine, based on your goals.

- Step Four: Put some things in place to help ensure success as you manage your habits.

Let's imagine your two primary goals are to: 1) Improve your fitness by working out three times a week, and 2) Lose five pounds in the next two months.

Step One

Assess your habits. We will label each one to determine if it helps, hurts, or plays a neutral role in helping you accomplish your goals.

- When you wake up in the morning, you brush your teeth (neutral).

- In the morning, you shuffle your feet to the kitchen where you make a cup of coffee (neutral).

- You make your bed (neutral).

- You take a shower (neutral).

- You go to work and grab a protein bar on the way out the door (hurts). (Sorry, but most protein bars are just candy bars.)

- You swing through the drive thru at Starbucks on your way to work to grab a latte (hurts).

- When you get home from work, you run on the treadmill for twenty minutes (helps).

- You have a healthy dinner of baked chicken and vegetables (helps).

- You watch TV for a couple of hours (neutral).

- You eat a bag of chips while you watch TV (hurts).

- You have a bowl of ice cream before you go to bed (hurts).

- You stay up watching TV until midnight (hurts).

- You wake up the next morning with just enough time to grab a protein bar for breakfast (hurts).

Your interpretation of helps, hurts, and neutral activities will be subjective. You may answer differently than me and that is okay. You get to be the boss of your assessment.

Step Two

Decide which habits you would like to eliminate from your life, based on your goals. In our example, the goals are to improve your fitness by working out three times a week and lose five pounds in the next two months.

Which habits will you likely eliminate?

- Grabbing a protein bar on the way out the door.

- Swinging through the drive thru at Starbucks on your way to work to grab a latte (perhaps this could become an occasional treat).

- Watching TV for more than two hours.

- Eating a bag of chips while you watch TV.

- Having a bowl of ice cream.

- Staying up watching TV until midnight.

- This may feel overwhelming all at once. You certainly can ease into the elimination of habits. You may choose to have ten potato chips instead of the bag, and you could have a couple of bites of ice cream. Or you may find it easier to quit something cold turkey. You may eliminate one "hurt" habit at a time, too, in order to ease into your new routines.

Step Three

Decide what habits you would like to add to your life, based on your goals.

- Wake up at an established time.

- Grab a banana on your way out the door in the morning.

- Establish Latte Thursdays (one latte per week).

- Watch TV a maximum of ninety minutes per night.

- Instead of a bag of chips, eat carrots and hummus to get the "crunch" (limit yourself to ¼ cup hummus).

- Replace ice cream with a sliced apple, heated in the microwave and sprinkled with some cinnamon and stevia.

- Go to bed by 11:00 P.M. to ensure seven hours of sleep.

Step Four

Put some things in place to ensure success.

- Stop buying protein bars, potato chips, and ice cream.

- Buy apples, bananas, carrots, and hummus.

- Choose a different route to work so you don't drive by Starbucks.

- Identify five shows you really enjoy watching, and limit your TV watching to those shows.

- Set your "go-to-bed" alarm for 11:00 P.M.

Record these ideas in your journal.

4. SET UP YOUR ENVIRONMENT

By creating habits, we start getting to some of the issues related to setting up your environment for success. For example, if you are trying to lose weight, then don't buy things that are tempting and not conducive to weight loss: protein bars, potato chips, and ice cream. It is a common practice for anyone starting a weight loss regime to begin by cleansing the kitchen of the bad foods. So, off go the ice cream, chips, and junk food of all kinds.

Setting up your environment is helpful for any goal you are trying to achieve.

- If you'd like to have greater peace and relaxation, you may choose to paint your walls a more soothing color and put candles in every room.

- If you'd like to watch less TV, you may choose to keep your TV in a room you use less often or keep it in a closed cabinet.

- If you'd like to lose weight, you can stop buying unhealthy foods.

- If you'd like to drink more water, you can put a glass of water on your night stand and drink it first thing in the morning.

- If you'd like to work out in the morning, you can set out your clothes the night before.

- If you'd like to floss your teeth every day, you can keep the floss next to your toothbrush.

- If you'd like to talk to your mom once a week, set a recurring alert on your calendar. This is called a passive reminder system. You log it in once, and then you don't have to think about it.

- If you would like to write in your journal every morning, create a cozy nook in your home that will inspire you. Light a candle, make a cup of tea or coffee, and settle in.

One of the things my husband likes to do is bring me things that I love. I love red velvet cake and chocolate of any kind. It was not unusual, in the past, to arrive home at the end of a day to find a full-on red velvet cake sitting on the counter. I don't know about you, but if the red velvet cake is in my house, it calls my name wherever I am. The same with chocolate. I finally had to ask my husband for help. I said, "It is so nice that you do this, and it means the world to me, but you have to understand, if it's in the house, I'm going to eat it. And I don't want to eat it." He reluctantly stopped buying sweet treats for me and switched to flowers. Perfect, because I love flowers. And I don't eat them.

I know you can't always control all aspects of your environment, especially if you have a family. When my kids were growing up, they, of course, wanted a reasonable amount of junk food. I could not say no to everything simply to manage my own lack of willpower. For the things they wanted that I particularly loved, I told them, "I'll get this for you, but you have to hide it." I know that sounds ridiculous, but "out of sight, out of mind" really does work to a degree. And I have to be honest about this, there were times I told my kids, "Seriously, you have to do a better job of hiding the junk food, especially the Swedish fish!"

Bottom line: do whatever it takes.

What can you change in your environment to set yourself up for success?

5. CREATE RITUALS AND ROUTINES

A collection of habits become a part of a ritual or a routine. For example, you may have a morning routine, as well as one during the evening.

As I have studied highly successful individuals, I have come to learn that morning and evening routines are typically key contributors to their success. Below are some of the most impactful elements you can incorporate into your morning or evening routines. I hope you will adopt some of these ideas.

Morning Routine:

- **Wake up early.** I'm talking about 4:00 A.M. or 5:00 A.M. This early hour is required for what follows.

- **Drink water.** Some women keep water on their night stand, and others simply make a trip to the water faucet as one of their first commitments of the day. Lemon water is a popular option.

- **Move.** Fifteen to ninety minutes will make a difference. This might be as relaxed as some stretching and yoga or as intense as sixty to ninety minutes of boot camp-style workouts.

- **Meditate.** For many individuals, this is as brief as five to ten minutes. Many use an app like Calm or Headspace. Every person who has shared their meditation experience has expressed greater productivity during the remainder of their day.

- **Journal.** This may involve capturing even a few thoughts in a journal or writing several thousand words of content. It may include listing things you are grateful for, what is on your mind today, or highlights from a chapter of a book.

- **Read.** Personal and professional growth is dependent on taking in knowledge. You may read a page a day or spend an hour reading. If you read five minutes a day, that adds up to thirty hours in a year. If you read an hour a day, that is 365 hours or 21,900 minutes!

6. TELL A FRIEND

Do you want to know how to hold yourself accountable? Start by telling someone else. Definitely. I know this is a real thing, because I have had times I did *not* tell anyone. It was terrible. I chose to not tell, so that I could bail!

Do you want help? Ask someone to be part of your accountability team.

For about six months, I gave up Diet Coke. I told some of my co-workers, because I'm most tempted to drink Diet Coke at work. And every time I go to the fridge, someone can see me. So, I asked them to provide accountability. "If you see me tip toeing to the fridge, trip me."

Maybe you want to limit yourself to only one glass of wine when you're socializing. Tell someone. "Hey, my goal is to limit myself to one glass of wine. I'm telling you, because I know my temptation is to have two or three. Will you remind me if I'm going in for a second?"

Or maybe you want to give up sugar. Tell someone. "Will you check in with me each day and remind me to not eat any sugar?" or "Can I reach out to you if I'm tempted to eat sugar?" or "Do you want to take on this challenge with me?"

7. SCHEDULE IT

Let's talk about your calendar. If you're like me, your calendar is a necessity. It is the assurance that you won't miss something important.

The million-dollar question, then, is "What qualifies as important?" Obligations involving other people almost always end up on a calendar. For most people, these things are important.

- A meeting with your team.

- A meeting with your boss.

- An interview with a new candidate.

- An after-hours networking event.

- Your son's baseball game.

- Your yoga class.

When it comes to ourselves, though, there are numerous things that we leave up to chance. We allow goals, wishes, and our regular to dos to whirl around in our head or on a list, willing them to somehow get accomplished. What might that list look like?

- Write a book

- Lose ten pounds.

- Read to my kids.

- Work out more regularly.

- Drink more water.

- Pay my bills.

- Eat healthy.

- Organize my house.

- Rake the leaves.

- Watch TV with my husband.

- Spend time with girlfriends.

I remember years of being overwhelmed because of all of the things I felt I should be doing. I was introduced to the concept of calendar blocking several years ago—and it helped tremendously. Calendar blocking is a process of putting the items from your to-do list onto your calendar. Using the list from above, this is how I might block these items on my calendar.

Keep in mind, some of these items would need planning and infrastructure to support the activity. I am illustrating the simple act of putting commitments onto a calendar.

Write a book
- Monday, Wednesday and Friday: 4:15 to 5:15 A.M. – "Write"

- Saturday: 7:00 to 9:00 A.M. – "Write"

Lose ten pounds
- Monday – Thursday: 6:30 P.M. – "Brush my teeth and do not eat any more food."

- Every morning: 6:00 A.M. – "Do not eat _____ today." Every day can be a different reminder (sugar, bread, crackers, chips, peanuts, etc.)

Read to my kids
- Tuesday, Thursday and Sunday evening: 6:30 to 7:30 P.M. – "Read with the kids"

Work out more regularly
- Monday through Thursday morning: 5:30 to 6:30 A.M. – "Go to the Gym"

Drink more water
- Add to morning and evening routine

Pay my bills
- Third Saturday morning of the month: 5:00 to 6:30 A.M. – "Pay bills"

Eat healthy
- Thursday evening: 9:00 to 10:00 P.M. (while watching TV with my husband) – "Order groceries online"
- Friday after work: 5:00 to 5:30 P.M. – "Pick up groceries"
- Sunday afternoon: 3:00 to 5:00 P.M. – "Prepare healthy food for the week"

Organize my house
- First Saturday of the month: 9:00 to 11:00 A.M. – "Clean out three drawers or closet shelves"

Rake the leaves
- The Second Saturday of October (every year) – "Rake Leaves"

Watch TV with my husband
- Monday through Friday evening: 8:30 to 9:45 P.M. – "Watch TV with Steve"

Spend time with girlfriends
- Every Thursday evening: 4:30 to 6:00 P.M. – "Schedule time with girlfriends"

Activities are scheduled daily, weekly, monthly, or annually, depending upon what they are. By creating these placeholders, I am able to meet with girlfriends fifty-two times over the course of a year. I am also able to enjoy the steady progress of getting drawers and closets cleaned out without being overwhelmed by trying to clean everything at once. And each year, as the leaves are falling, I don't have to feel overwhelmed every day. I have my raking day blocked off.

It's also possible to include relaxed multitasking in your scheduled activities. The seventy-five minutes of watching TV has multiple purposes. It is time Steve really enjoys, it is relaxation and winding down time for me, and it is entertainment. It is also finite. At 9:45, I launch my evening routine and am in bed by 10:15 for an early wake up.

The beauty of calendar blocking is that you won't have to feel overwhelmed by your day-to-day life, because everything is accounted for.

You can exercise flexibility in your schedule. You'll find that you waste much less time and accomplish more, because you have committed to the things in life that matter to you. You are taking ownership and responsibility to live your best life and to be the best version of yourself.

How will you ensure progress?

Going back to the concept of New Year's Resolutions, remember that more than three-quarters of us don't make it past the first month. So, what can you do to measure your progress?

Below are five ideas:

1. ESTABLISH A DEADLINE FOR COMPLETION

Most goals can be inspired by a deadline. Deadlines create healthy stress by giving you something to strive for. When you have a deadline, it requires you to have a plan, establish milestones, add items to your to-do list, and get to work. Striving toward improvement is one of the things that helps us feel fully alive.

By what date do you want to:

- Paint your bedroom?
- Clean out all of your closets?
- Host a movie night for your friends?
- Lose eight pounds?

Some goals may not have a deadline. You may have a goal to give up sugar. This is a habit you will incorporate into your daily routines.

2. ESTABLISH MILESTONES

Most of your goals will require steps to advance. Milestones may be similar to items on a to-do list.

This will depend upon your goal—and they can be put on your calendar so you know if you're on track to meet your goal completion deadline.

- If you want to lose eight pounds, your first milestone may be your half-way point.

- If you want to clean out all of your closets, a milestone may be when you've tackled the first one. (You may also notice the process wasn't as bad as you expected.)

- If you want to paint your bedroom, a milestone may be selecting the color and buying the paint. (You can look at the project as a series of steps. "Okay, I've got that completed. The next milestone will be to tape off the room. Then, I'll paint.")

- If you want to give up sugar, you may look at your first day, your first week, and your first month as key milestones.

3. CELEBRATE ALONG THE WAY

Milestones and mini-accomplishments are worth celebrating.

Find a way to celebrate each step and small win along the way. If you've made it a full week with no sugar, that's fantastic. How can you celebrate? You can simply acknowledge it to yourself, you could write it in your journal in big red letters, or you can tell a friend. You can't, however, celebrate, by treating yourself to a big piece of cake. You may opt for a savory treat you've come to appreciate in your sugar-free journey.

If you've got your paint color selected and purchased, check it off your list. (Doesn't it feel *so* good to put a checkmark on your to-do list?)

I love the celebration of a newly cleaned closet. It is simply looking at it every time you find an excuse to walk past. Don't you agree?

4. MAINTAIN A MASTER LIST

One of the things I've alluded to throughout the book is the challenge of managing so many areas of life. If you want to live the kind of life where you are continually growing, you need a list of some kind. There is no way around it.

Your master list (or a vision board) could include your big goals for the current year. It could also contain all of your to-dos for the month or quarter. It could also have a section for areas of focus during this decade of your life.

You get to decide how to create and maintain your list. But remember, if you don't have one at all, you are leaving too much of your potential on the table.

5. FORGIVE YOURSELF ON THE JOURNEY

This one is a big one.

As you move forward with goals and plans, you will experience successes along the way. You will also have setbacks. There will be days you don't accomplish what you want to. You'll eat sugar after a thirty-day streak, you'll gain five pounds on vacation in the middle of your weight loss plan, you'll yell at your kids, and you'll be disrespectful to a friend. You will have days you want nothing more than to lie in bed with the covers over your head and—on some days—you will feel like all of this is for naught.

All of these things, and many more, will happen along the way. This is predictable, expected, and perfectly, amazingly OKAY.

Each day is a new day. Get back on track when you're ready. Setbacks are a part of every plan.

I know you have a next best place within you. Where is it? What will you do?

The end of this book is a beginning. I encourage you to revisit your life, on purpose, every year or even more often whenever life demands a new set of resolutions.

I hope you will check out the information on the following pages to get in touch and join my growing tribe of women on fire.

Most importantly, I hope you experience an amazing life this year and the years to come. I can't wait to see you SPARK!

WHERE DO YOU GO FROM HERE?

I appreciate you more than you know.

Reading this book is a starting point. Thank you, by the way. As you move forward, I would love to remain part of your support team. You have options!

My services are designed to help YOU increase your happiness, confidence and sense of purpose. You'll notice a strong focus on fostering positivity and productivity in your day-to-day life.

I've learned over the years that different things resonate with different women.

Don't be overwhelmed by the options. As you read the list, just check in with one or two options that resonate with you (or intrigue you!) Remember, I'm a short-list person. Start with **one** thing.

- ☐ Download the Women Who Spark resource guide for completing the exercises in this book: www.womenwhosparkbooks.com

- ☐ Sign up for my *Women Who Spark Boot Camp.* (www.aletanorris.com/shop/boot-camp)

- ☐ Take the *Women Who Spark Life Assessment.* (www.aletanorris.com/shop/ women-who-spark-life-assessment)

- ☐ Visit my Tribe page and introduce yourself to me. (www.aletanorris.com/tribe)

- ☐ Need some coaching support to find your spark, and perhaps cope with challenges? I'm your gal! (www.aletanorris.com/shop/coaching)

- ☐ You can join my Facebook community, the *Women Who Spark Tribe.* (www.aletanorris.com/tribe)

Please let me know how I can help you, my friend.

Aleta xo

Women Who Spark Life Assessment

Assess 10 areas of your life, then create your plan for a future that sparks!

Take an important step toward making your life all it can be. If you want to take control of your happiness, cultivate confidence, and find purpose in your life, you're on the right path.

The purpose of this assessment is to create space for you to think about your life. Let's face it, in our busy, overwhelming lives, we spend our time getting stuff done. We don't use that time to step back and think about how life is going for us.

This is your opportunity!

Don't risk leaving your future up to chance—and don't let the rest of us miss out on the best of who you are meant to be.

Your report will include your results, a working section to brainstorm strategies for your priority areas, and even a list of ideas to help you brainstorm.

Visit www.aletanorris.com/shop/women-who-spark-life-assessment for details!

Women Who Spark Boot Camp

Join this eight-week Boot Camp to design an amazing year *and* a future defined by purpose and passion!

What will you experience?

- Eight weeks of content, including 30 video lessons, supported by a workbook to help you track your progress and plan your future.

- Small group coaching support.

- Your "Women Who Spark" Life Assessment.

- Camaraderie with other women on the exact same journey inside a private Facebook community.

- Bonuses!

Visit www.aletanorris.com/shop/boot-camp for all of the details!

ACKNOWLEDGMENTS

I have been blessed by so many people in my life. Every person I mention here contributed significantly to the themes of this book: happiness, confidence, and purpose. I am grateful to each and every one of you mentioned below. The difficulty is that I am grateful for so many people beyond these pages. If you are not mentioned here, and if our paths have crossed, you are important to me.

To my husband, Steve. You patiently supported me as I spent hours and hours pouring over a manuscript I barely knew how to write without ever complaining once. Thank you for supporting my dream to build a business to encourage women.

To Uber Eats. You ensure my husband is fed on all the days I am hidden away in my office—which is a lot.

To all of my children—Jaimie, Ben (and my new daughter-in-law, Kelsey), Steph, Joe, and Haley. You bring Steve and me countless moments of joy. You are our best friends in the world and our happiest moments are when we are with you and the important people in your lives.

To my grandparents, Loren and Bertha Mae. You were the kindest, most loving people I had in my life. You are the inspiration behind my addiction to patience, kindness, and calmness. As you taught me, Grandma, every person is doing the best they can. I love that belief in people. And Grandpa, thank you for all the times you rolled out the red carpet for me.

To my dad, Paul, and stepmom, Linda. We didn't start as joyfully as the Brady Bunch, but we figured it out. Thank you for raising a blended family of six kids and for supporting every one of us in our passions and endeavors. You paved the way for my own experiences in a blended family.

To my little sister, Sherri. You have been my number one fan for more than fifty years. With all of my imperfections, you have never faltered once. Not many people get that level of dedication. I am grateful for you beyond measure. You are woven into the fabric of this book.

To Nancy, my Living As A Leader business partner and dear friend of over twenty-five years. We have impacted many lives through our work. Our journey together, anchored by our friendship, has been a blessing.

To Uncle Carl and Aunt Lois. Thank you so much for my happiness as a child, and especially the fudge bars and Dreamsicles. I miss both of you and appreciate your contribution to my happiness and confidence today.

To my zany girlfriend group—Kathleen, Leslie, Mary, LeighAnn, Anne, Lisa, Tina, and Molls. While my kids were growing up, I loved Friends! I dreamed one day of hanging out with my friends every day at a coffee shop like they did. I love that we have that. Not the coffee shop part, but the hanging out with wine part. (Much better!) You bring a level of laughter and joy into my life that I am not capable of cultivating on my own. Oh, and thank you for being just enough of a disaster that I get to practice my stuff on you.

To Katie Brazelton, my coach. I was inspired to be you when I read *Pathway to Purpose for Women.* Thank you for sharing your vulnerability, along with the imperfections of your life journey, in your book. I needed that when I was at my most difficult moment in life to know I was not the only person who had created what felt like a disaster. And, more than that, thank you for believing so vehemently in my future when I could not see it myself.

To Teri Capshaw, my editor and unexpected co-writer. Teri, your patience and literary excellence have become a critical part of my book. After a pain-staking line-by-line edit of this book, you embraced my idea that, if we started over from the beginning, you could turn my words into something more impressive. You have done that in spades. It has been sheer joy to work with you on this project. I can't wait for our next book.

To Kary Oberbrunner and the Igniting Souls Tribe. Kary, Author Academy Elite is amazing. Thank you so much for turning your experiences of how to write, publish, and launch a book into a business to help the rest of us. I am immensely grateful for your detailed process, your coaching support, and the encouragement of your Tribe. I don't see how this book would exist without you.

To Reji Laberje, my other editor, book launch manager and newfound friend. Thank you for crafting the very creative and enjoyable journey leading up to my book launch date. Wow, it takes a lot of people to help an author write and launch a book.

To the many, many, many, too-many-to-count women I have had the honor and joy of knowing over the decades. I have enjoyed your friendship, along with your stories of success and struggle. Thank you for all of the things you have taught me over the years. You are an inspiration to me.

BOOK CLUB
DISCUSSION GUIDE

A woman needs her tribe! Chatting about things with others often makes the difference. Your girlfriend group or book club can be your friendly accountability team. If you talk about it out loud, it is more likely to take hold.

This book is not meant to be entertainment. Well, not exactly. Maybe a titch entertaining. Mostly, it's work. And, you are worth it to do the work.

You can approach your discussion group in a couple of different ways. If you'd like to take on a comprehensive approach, you can have everyone in the group take the Women Who Spark Life Assessment (aletanorris. com/shop) and discuss the book step-by-step, along with your assessment results.

Or, you can take on a more holistic approach and talk about the book in one or two conversations and skip the assessment. I've provided discussion questions for both approaches.

YOUR COMPREHENSIVE APPROACH

1. **Women Who Spark Life Assessment:**

   a. What did you learn from your results?

   b. What three priorities are you going to focus on?

   c. What is your strategy for each of your priorities?

2. **Part One: Your Foundation**

   a. What have you come to know more clearly about yourself?

   b. What have you uncovered from your past that you need to let go of?

   c. What areas of your life are going best for you?

   d. What areas are disappointing you?

3. **Part Two: Find Your Sparks**

   a. What simple things make you happy?

   b. What "I'll be happy when" will you let go of?

   c. What is getting in the way of your confidence?

   d. What will you do to become more confident?

   e. What disappointments have been affecting you?

   f. What will you do to deal with disappointment?

4. **Part Three: Make Everything Brighter**

   a. What are you doing to make someone else's day?

   b. What are you doing to make your day?

   c. What are you doing to rob yourself or others of joy?

   d. In what ways can you more successfully remain calm in your life?

5. **Part Four: Discover Your Bigger Purpose**

   a. What seeds have been stirring in you over time?

   b. What would you love to do that you haven't acted on yet?

   c. What is your first step?

   d. In what way does fear get in your way?

   e. What can you do to move beyond fear?

   f. What do you want to focus on?

   g. What needs your attention on the operations side of your life?

   h. What special purpose or passion would you like to advance?

   i. What is your first step toward advancing this purpose or passion?

6. **Your Final Thought:** Where do you go from here?

A MORE HOLISTIC APPROACH

1. What were the key take-aways for you as you read through *Women Who Spark?*

2. What did you learn about yourself?

3. What two areas of your life do you want to focus on?

4. What is your strategy to approach your areas for improvement?

5. What passion or dream is percolating within you?

6. What first (or next) steps will you take to advance your passion or dream?

ENDNOTES

1   Freeman, Dr. Arthur and DeWolf, Rose, *Would,
    Coulda, Shoulda: Overcoming Regrets, Mistakes and
    Missed Opportunities,* (Harper Perennial, New
    York, 1989), p. 31

2   Klein, Carole and Gotti, Richard, *Overcoming
    Regret: Lessons From The Roads Not Taken,*
    (Bantam Books, New York, 1992), p. ix

3   Bach, David, *Start Late, Finish Rich* (Broadway,
    New York, 2005).

4   Covey, Stephen, *The Seven Habits of Highly
    Effective People,* (Simon & Schuster, New York,
    1989), p. 79.

5   Burnett, Bill and Evans, Dave, *Designing Your
    Life: How to Build A Well-Lived, Joyful Life,*
    (Alfred A. Knopf, New York, 2017), pp. 4, 5.

6   Soot, Amit, M.D., Healthy habits that boost happiness, Mayo Clinic Website, accessed March 15, 2019 (https://www.mayoclinic. org/healthy-lifestyle/adult-health/in-depth/ healthy-habits-that-boost-happiness/ art-20267401).

7   Rubin, Gretchen, *The Happiness Project* (Harper, New York, 2009).

8   Professor Steven Hayes (some insecurity and self doubt is good).

9   Hebrews 11:1, New International Version.

10   Jeremiah 29:11, New International Version.

11   Wagner, David, *Life as a Daymaker: how to change the world by making someone's day* (Jodere Group, San Diego, 2002).

12   Covey, Stephen, *The Seven Habits of Highly Effective People* (Simon & Schuster, New York, 1989), p. 105.

13   Brown, Brené, *Braving the Wilderness: The Quest for True Belonging and the Courage to Stand Alone* (Random House, New York, 2017).

14   Brazelton, Katie, *Pathway To Purpose For Women* (Zondervan, Grand Rapids, 2005).

15   Brown, Brené, *Braving the Wilderness: The Quest for True Belonging and the Courage to Stand Alone* (Random House, New York, 2017).

SPARK NOTE!
What Will YOU Ignite On?

Spark Note!

Ignite On: Your Spark

"When you gain the confidence to stop looking around - and start working on you - everything will change."
~ Aleta Norris